*A CREATIVE STEP-BY-STEP GUIDE TO*

# GARDEN
# PROJECTS

A CREATIVE STEP-BY-STEP GUIDE TO

# GARDEN
# PROJECTS

Author
## Mike Lawrence

Photographer
## Neil Sutherland

 AURA BOOKS

CLB 4540
This edition published in 1997 by Aura Books
© 1996 CLB International, Godalming, Surrey
Printed and bound in Singapore
All rights reserved
ISBN 0-94779-322-7

## Credits

Edited and designed: Ideas into Print
Photographs: Neil Sutherland
Typesetting: Ideas into Print
Production Director: Gerald Hughes
Production: Ruth Arthur, Sally Connolly, Neil Randles,
Karen Staff

## THE AUTHOR

**Mike Lawrence** has been writing about home and garden
improvements for over 20 years, contributing articles
regularly to all the major magazines in this field. He has
also written or contributed to over 40 books, has edited
three major practical partwork collections, and for seven
long years answered listeners' questions about home
improvement topics every Saturday morning on one of
London's independent radio stations. He learned his craft
the hard way, after moving his young family from a
cramped modern box into an old farmhouse that had
never seen a home improvement since the day it was built.
After saving it for posterity - a job that took 18 years - he
moved to a new house in a vain attempt to escape 'doing-
it-himself' forever, and found a virgin plot badly in need of
some creative garden projects instead.

## THE PHOTOGRAPHER

**Neil Sutherland** has more than 25 years experience in a
wide range of photographic fields, including still-life,
portraiture, reportage, natural history, cookery, landscape
and travel. His work has been published in countless books
and magazines throughout the world.

*Half-title page: Bricks are an ideal material for making a
raised bed, here home to a magnificent rhododendron.*

*Title page: Wooden decking is a relatively easy and
effective way of creating an attractive patio surface.*

*Copyright page: A simple picket fence painted a subtle
blue-gray, not only marks a boundary, but also forms a
charming backdrop to a bed of annual flowers.*

# CONTENTS

# THE FRAMEWORK OF YOUR GARDEN

There is more to creating the garden you want than simply planting things. For a start, you will need to enclose your property, partly for security reasons but mainly to give yourself a fixed framework within which to plant the garden itself. This means putting up fences of one type or another, or else building some sturdy boundary walls. The method of enclosure you choose can become a major feature of the garden's appearance if you wish, or can be made to blend unobtrusively into the background as your planting plans mature. Next, your garden will need some hard surfaces - patios, decks, paths and even steps if the site slopes - to allow you to sit outside and move about freely, especially when the ground itself is wet. These all have a decorative as well as a functional purpose, so care is needed to plan and design them to last. Three-dimensional structures, such as pergolas and rose arches, create attractive visual features in their own right, breaking up the garden layout and allowing you to display climbing plants to perfection. Lastly, no garden would be complete without a range of simpler features, from seats and planters to cold frames and bird tables. So whether you are remodeling your garden on the grand scale or simply adding smaller features to an existing scheme, the range of projects in this book should give you plenty of food for thought.

**Left:** *Wooden decking complements a garden pond.*     **Above:** *A simple garden bench.*

# Laying slabs on sand

The quickest way to lay a garden path or patio surface is to bed paving slabs on a sand bed. The slabs are relatively large, so once you have prepared the site you can quickly cover a sizeable area. The first step is to choose your slabs and make a note of their size and thickness. Most slabs are squares or rectangles; square slabs range in size from 9 or 12in(230 or 305mm) up to 24in(610mm) across, while rectangles measure from 9x18in (230x455mm) to 18x27in(455x685mm). The larger slabs are quite heavy and you may need help to handle them. Some ranges of paving also offer interlocking hexagonal slabs, complete with two types of half hexagon for finishing off the edges of the paved area, and slabs with a quadrant cutout in one corner; four of these placed together create a circular opening to fit round a tree or other feature. Most slabs are made in shades of buff, red and gray; the surface texture may be smooth, textured, riven to resemble natural split stone, or embossed in imitation of stone setts or paving bricks. Once you have selected your slabs, mark out the site with pegs and string lines so that you can take measurements and draw up a simple scale plan. This will be invaluable for estimating materials accurately and is a useful laying guide if you intend to create a pattern using slabs of different colors. Then you can clear and excavate the site, provide an edge restraint to stop sand from leaching out and start laying the slabs.

*5 The paving should have a slight fall (away from the house if this is adjacent) to help rainwater to run off it. Use a batten and spirit level to check the direction of the fall.*

*1 Unless your subsoil is firm, you will need to spread and compact a layer of solid material over the site. Gravel or crushed rock is ideal.*

*2 Excavate the site to the required depth, level the subsoil and spread a 3in(75mm)-thick layer of the filling. Compact it with a length of fence post.*

*3 Shovel out the bedding sand on top of the compacted filling and rake it out evenly to a depth of 1-2in(25-50mm) across the site.*

*4 If you have edge restraints, use a notched batten to level the sand so its surface is just less than the slab thickness below the top of the edging.*

**6** Start by laying just four slabs in one corner of the site, setting small wooden spacers between adjacent slabs to ensure an even gap for the pointing.

**7** Lay a batten across the slabs and check the fall direction. Tamp the slabs further into the sand bed if necessary, using the handle of a club hammer.

You can remove the wooden spacers as soon as each slab is surrounded by other slabs.

**8** Continue laying slabs across the site, kneeling on a board on the sand bed if you cannot reach right across the area from the edge. Check the fall regularly as you work.

**9** Remove the last spacers and spread some fine sand across the surface. Brush it well into all the joints with a soft-bristled broom, then sweep off the excess.

# Block pavers on sand

Block pavers are relative newcomers to the world of garden building, but have rapidly become extremely popular because they are small and easy to handle, are designed to be dry-laid on a sand bed and need no pointing. Unlike other dry-laid paving, they can even withstand the weight of motor vehicles thanks to the way they interlock once laid, so they can be used for all hard surfaces around the garden. However, you must lay the sand bed with a continuous edge restraint to prevent the sand from leaching out. The blocks are made in a wide range of colors and generally rectangular in shape, measuring 4x8in(100x200mm) and about 2½in(65mm) thick. This shape allows you to lay the blocks in a variety of patterns, from a simple stretcher-bond arrangement resembling brickwork to herringbone and basketweave designs. You can also lay them diagonally across the area you are paving, filling in the edges with cut-to-size pieces. If the pattern requires many cut blocks, it is well worth hiring a hydraulically operated block splitter that cuts cleanly through the dense aggregate. You *can* split them with a bolster chisel and a club hammer, but they may not break cleanly.

*3 Decide on the laying pattern you intend to follow and start placing the first blocks on the sand bed. For a patio or path, simply tamp the blocks down level with each other using a hammer handle.*

*1 Start by placing edge restraints - pegged boards or curbstones, for example - all round the area you intend to pave. Then cover it with sand and level it roughly with a straightedge.*

*2 To get the blocks level with the top of the edge restraints, measure the block thickness and tamp the sand down to this depth. Then check that it has a very slight fall across the area.*

*Use concreting sand for the bedding layer, as building sand is too soft and may stain the blocks.*

4 Most patterns have a plain border. Here, a single row is laid along each edge. Use a batten and spirit level to check that the second edge is level.

5 Start laying the blocks in your chosen pattern; this will be a simple basketweave design with pairs of blocks placed at right angles.

6 Build up the paving by adding more blocks, working away from the first corner. Check constantly that the pattern is correct as you work.

Tamp down any pavers that stand proud.

7 After completing a small area, use a straightedge to check that the blocks are level with each other. Then check the fall with your spirit level.

8 When you have completed all the paving, spread some fine sand over the surface and brush it well into all the joints between the blocks before sweeping off the excess.

# Variations on a theme

The block paver is ideal for creating paths, patios and other paved areas in the garden, because it is light and easy to handle and quick and simple to lay. Most people go for a monochrome effect, laying pavers of just one color and relying on the way in which they are placed for extra visual interest. However, as pavers are made to a standard size there is no reason why you should not use pavers of different colors to create distinctive patterns, or even mix them with other paving materials such as slabs (see page 18) or cobbles. Pavers now come in a wide range of shades, from yellow and red to buff and brown and also in various shades of gray, so you can choose complementary or contrasting effects as you prefer. The only limit to what you can create is your own imagination. One of the simplest options, illustrated on the opposite page, is to use a band of different-colored pavers along the edges of the area. If you prefer to mix the colors across the whole area, you can simply insert pavers of the second color regularly or at random. The basketweave pattern - pairs of pavers laid at right angles to the adjoining pair - allows you to create a checkerboard effect, while the popular herringbone pattern can feature zigzagging bands of different-colored pavers. If you are prepared to cut blocks in half, there is even more scope for creating attractive patterns. Keep an eye open for unusual effects created with block pavers in public spaces; you can then copy any ideas you like in your own garden.

**Above:** *You can lay block pavers and frostproof paving bricks round gentle curves by interspersing cut units amongst the whole ones. This path is bedded on mortar and has its joints left open.*

*1 First work out the pattern you intend to lay on squared paper, so that you can order the right numbers of each color. Start building up the pattern from one edge, checking it against your plan as you work.*

*Block pavers are relatively easy to cut cleanly by hand, but a hired block splitter makes cutting child's play.*

*2 Here, half blocks in a contrasting color have been used to fill in the open center of a square formed by four full blocks. The resulting motif is repeated all the way across the area to create a striking visual effect.*

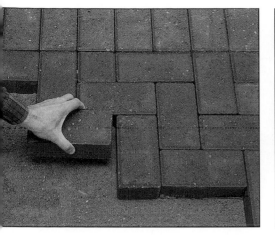

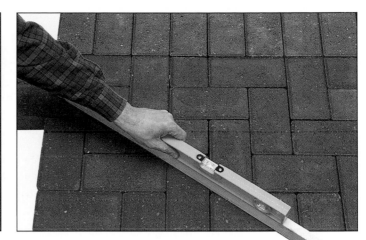

*1* A contrasting border is one of the simplest and most attractive effects you can create. Here, the border pavers are laid side by side and the infill is added in herringbone style.

*2* Tamp the pavers into the sand bed, using a wood offcut and a club hammer to set them level with their neighbors. Lift and relay any that sink too low or stand proud.

*3* Use a long wooden straightedge and a spirit level to check that there is a slight fall across the paved area. This will ensure that heavy rain can drain freely off the surface.

**Below:** *Try mixing materials as well as colors. Here pavers in two colors are interspersed with slabs to form paths leading to a brick 'roundabout'.*

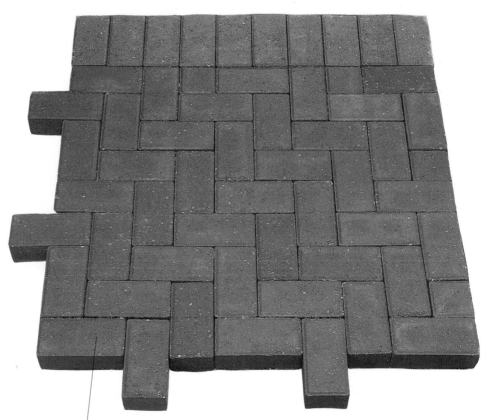

Herringbone paving can be laid in one color, as here, or by mixing blocks of different colors and surface textures.

*4* The continuous pattern begins to build up as you work across the area. The cut blocks at the edges of the area maintain the herringbone bond.

# Using pavers with slabs

The idea of mixing pavers of different colors can create even more dramatic effects if you are prepared to work to a diagonal grid rather than a square one. This will allow you to create straight lines or zigzags running at an angle to the edge of the paved area, according to the laying pattern you decide to adopt. However, you must remember that designs of this sort involve a great deal of block cutting at the perimeter of the area, so allow for this when estimating quantities and add some extra pavers to cater for the occasional cutting blunder. It is a good idea to plan the layout and pattern carefully on paper first, so that you can check your progress as you work and avoid misplacing any elements of the pattern.

An alternative to creating patterns with pavers of different colors is to mix them with other paving materials. Small paving slabs look particularly attractive when used in this way, appearing like stepping stones across a background of contrasting color. Be sure to choose your slabs with care so that their size coordinates with a whole number of pavers, or you will end up either with unacceptably wide joints or impossibly intricate block trimming. Since pavers measure a standard 4x8in(100x200mm), you can lay them with slabs having sides measuring 12, 24 or 36in (305, 610 or 915mm), but not with other sizes. Remember, too, that garden paving slabs are usually only about 1½in(38mm) thick, compared with the 2-2½in (50-65mm) of the block pavers, so you will need to compensate by placing extra sand beneath the slabs as you lay them.

1 *After fixing the edge restraints and placing the border pavers, start building up the diagonal pattern. Use a string line that you can move across the area as the pattern extends, and include pavers cut at an angle as necessary to maintain the pattern.*

*As the pattern extends, check that the exposed corners of the pavers are aligned and at right angles to the border.*

2 *The simple gray zigzag perfectly complements the straight border. Here it is about to be repeated at the near edge of a path. Hire a block splitter to make light work of cutting the angled infill pieces neatly.*

1 *If you are mixing pavers and slabs, choose slabs with sides equal to a whole number of pavers. Place extra sand beneath the slabs to keep them level with the pavers.*

2 *A square arrangement of slabs and pavers has a pleasing symmetry. Experiment with other patterns on paper first, to check that they will work in practice.*

**Left:** *Here, slabs and pavers are mixed on a larger scale, with bands three pavers wide framing squares of four smooth slabs. For extra variety, the pavers have been laid in running bond, with cut pieces inserted as necessary where the bands intersect.*

**Right:** *A band of weathered paving bricks laid on edge contrasts well with the color and texture of the paving slabs that flank it. The slabs hold the bricks securely in place.*

*Below: The standard mortar mix for general-purpose bricklaying consists of one part of ordinary Portland cement, one part of hydrated lime and six parts of fine sand. You can use masonry cement instead of cement and lime or replace the lime with a chemical plasticizer.*

# Mortar and concrete

Mortar and concrete are the essential raw materials for all sorts of garden projects. Mortar is a mixture of cement, hydrated lime, fine sand and water and is used as an adhesive to bond bricks and blocks together when building walls and steps, or to bed paving materials on a solid substrate. The lime makes the mortar easier to work than a plain cement/sand mix, and prevents shrinkage and cracking as the mortar dries. It can be replaced in the mix by a liquid chemical plasticizer that you add to the water before making up the mortar. Alternatively, use special masonry cement that already contains a plasticizer instead of ordinary Portland cement and lime; mix one part of this cement to five parts of sand. Concrete mixes are used to form drives, paths, patios and steps or to create a solid foundation for walls and garden buildings. It is the sand that gives the mortar its final color, so use the same sand throughout each job. For a light-colored mortar, use pale sand and white cement. Concrete for in-ground use is a mix of one part cement, $2\frac{1}{2}$ parts coarse sand and $3\frac{1}{2}$ parts aggregate. If you are using 'all-in' aggregate, use one part of cement to five parts of aggregate. Dry, ready-mixed mortar or concrete to which you add water is ideal for small jobs, but comparatively expensive for larger projects.

Fine sand (6 parts)

Portland cement (1 part)

Hydrated lime (1 part)

1 Measure out the dry ingredients by volume and pile them up on a smooth hard surface. A board offcut is ideal for mixing small quantities.

2 Start to mix the ingredients together by turning them over with a shovel. Work from the edges of the heap towards the center.

3 If the sand is at all damp, lumps will form within the mix. Break them up as you work using the edge of the shovel in a chopping motion.

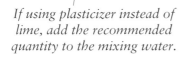

*If using plasticizer instead of lime, add the recommended quantity to the mixing water.*

**4** *When the mix is a uniform color and free from lumps, form a crater in the center of the heap and add a little water from a watering can or hose.*

**5** *Shovel the dry mix from the edges of the heap into the crater so that it absorbs the water. Turn the mix over and add more water as necessary to create a mix of uniform consistency for bricklaying, but take care not to make it too sloppy.*

**6** *The mix is the right consistency if it is firm enough to hold its shape when formed into smooth ridges with the shovel. If it is too sloppy, add one small measure of both cement and lime and five equal measures of sand to the mix to absorb the excess water.*

**7** *Compact the mix into a neat heap with the back of the spade so that it does not dry out too quickly. Test its plasticity by taking a slice of mortar onto your trowel; it should stick readily to the blade.*

## Concrete mixes

Use only ordinary Portland cement, not masonry cement, to make concrete. You can buy coarse sand and aggregate separately or ready-mixed as combined aggregate. The maximum aggregate size should not exceed $^3/_4$in (20mm). Keep all materials dry before mixing them.

If you are using combined aggregates, mix one part of cement to five parts of aggregate, measured by volume.

**Right:** Mix the dry ingredients thoroughly. Add water to form a mix that just holds its shape on the shovel.

With separate sand and gravel, use $3^1/_2$ parts of gravel and $2^1/_2$ parts of sand to 1 part of cement.

Combined aggregate (5 parts)

Portland cement (1 part)

$^3/_4$in(20mm) gravel or crushed rock ($3^1/_2$ parts)

Portland cement (1 part)

Coarse sand ($2^1/_2$ parts)

# Laying slabs on mortar

Slabs laid on a sand bed are ideal for a patio or path, but will subside and crack if you drive a vehicle over them. A paved drive must be much more substantial, so excavate the site to a depth of at least 6in(150mm) - more if the subsoil is unstable - and lay a concrete base a minimum of 4in(100mm) thick. You can use ready-mixed concrete or mix your own with one part of cement to five parts of combined sand and ¾in(20mm) aggregate. Set up wooden shuttering around the area to give the base a neat square edge, tamp the concrete down well, level the surface with a long straightedge laid across the formwork and remove any excess material. Give the base a slight fall across its width, and incorporate full-width vertical expansion joints of hardboard or similar material every 10ft(3m) to prevent the base from cracking. Cover with plastic against rain or frost, or use damp sacking if it is hot and sunny. Leave to set for at least three days.

*Use a spirit level and a long straightedge to check level and fall.*

**2** *Lower each slab gently onto its mortar bed and tamp it down with the handle of a club hammer to compress the mortar and make the slab level with its neighbors.*

*Use a fairly sloppy mortar mix so that it is easy to spread beneath the slabs.*

**1** *To give the slabs adequate support, place the mortar on the concrete base in a square beneath the edges of the slab and add more mortar beneath the center of the slab.*

**3** After placing the slab, bedding it down and setting it to the correct fall, insert small wooden spacers between it and its neighbors to ensure an even pointing gap.

**4** Continue laying the slabs in this way, checking that the surface has the correct fall. Tamp down out-of-line slabs a little more if necessary.

Use a mortar mix of 1 part cement, 1 part lime (or a measure of plasticizer) and 6 parts building sand.

Use a concrete mix of 1 part cement, 2½ parts concreting sand and 3½ parts ¾in(20mm) aggregate or a mix of 1 part cement to 5 parts of combined aggregates.

**Below:** To encourage grass, moss and plants between the slabs, lay them with wider-than-usual joints and fill these with soil instead of pointing them with mortar.

**5** When all the slabs are laid and leveled, remove the wooden spacers and point the joints with a fairly dry mix. Force it well into the joints with the edge of a pointing trowel.

## A pointing guide

If the pointing mortar stains the slab surface as you work, reduce the problem by using a guide - a plywood offcut with a slot cut in it to match the joint width. Fill the joints through the slot.

23

# Crazy paving

Crazy paving aptly describes the effect created when pieces of randomly shaped stone are interlocked to create a hard surface for drives, paths and patios. It is economical to buy, making use as it does of broken pieces of square or rectangular paving that would otherwise go to waste. The stones fit together like the pieces of a jigsaw and the gaps between them are pointed with mortar, which bonds the stones to a stable base layer. An old concrete surface would make an ideal foundation for a driveway or parking place; well-rammed coarse aggregate is suitable for light-duty areas, such as a patio or garden path. Crazy paving can look very attractive if you fit the pieces together carefully and neatly detail the pointing. You can achieve interesting decorative effects by mixing stones of different hues and textures or by using mortar pigments in the pointing that contrast with the colors of the stones. Having trimmed the stones, if necessary, to improve their fit, piece them together one by one, tamp them down into a mortar bed and level them. Start at the perimeter, using stones with one straight side, and use a long wooden straightedge as you lay down more stones to ensure that they are level. If necessary, check that the stones are laid to a slight fall to allow surface water to drain off.

*1 A solid concrete or well-rammed aggregate foundation is essential. Spread a bed of fairly sloppy mortar along the perimeter of the base layer.*

*2 Choose relatively large stones with two adjacent straight edges to form the corners of square or rectangular paved areas.*

*3 Set the corner stone in place, tamp it down into the mortar bed using a wood offcut to protect the surface and check the levels in both directions.*

*Small pieces are ideal for awkward spaces.*

## Preparing stones

*When the load of stone is delivered, sort it out into groups: corner stones with two adjacent square edges, perimeter stones with one straight edge, large, irregularly shaped stones and smaller infill pieces.*

*Right: To break up a stone or improve the fit, sandwich it between two stones and crack it with a firm hammer blow.*

**4** Place the next perimeter stone on the mortar bed in line with the corner stone, tamp it down and check that it lies level with its neighbor.

**5** Complete one edge of the area, including the next corner stone. Then start building up the jigsaw effect with large and smaller stones.

**6** As you extend the area of paving, use a spirit level and a long wood straightedge to check that the stones are level (or have a constant fall).

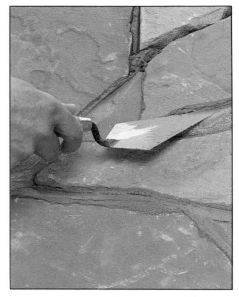

**7** Allow the mortar bed to harden overnight. Fill and point the joints. Draw the trowel point along the joint to leave a ridge and two sloping bevels.

**Below:** Gravel makes an attractive alternative to pointed joints if the stones are large or do not fit closely together. Low plants flourish in the gaps. Bed in individual stones in mortar to ensure their stability.

Allow a slope of 1 in 40 away from adjacent buildings or across free-standing paths and drives.

# Edges, tiles and slabs

You do not have to restrict yourself to standard paving and edging materials when it comes to creating paths and other paved areas in your garden. One material that has become popular again in recent years is terracotta, an unglazed red-brown material made from clay, fine sand and sometimes pulverized pottery waste. It was a favorite of Victorian builders and gardeners and is used nowadays to make plain pavers, embossed tiles and a variety of decorative edgings, including the traditional Victorian-style rope edging. As long as the material is declared by its manufacturers to be frostproof, it can be used safely out of doors in all climates. You can use it on its own for a striking monochrome effect, or mix it with other paving and edging materials to create areas of strong visual contrast, such as the herringbone path shown on page 27.

It is best to bed terracotta pavers and tiles on a continuous mortar bed; the material is not as strong as other paving materials, so it needs solid support underneath. Edging and matching decorative corner posts should also be set in mortar; this should be sloped away at each side to allow the paving material to be laid right up to the edging, leaving just the decorative rope part exposed. As well as terracotta, frostproof ceramic tiles can also be used in the garden. They work best on a small scale, perhaps as a path edging or to provide a splash of color and pattern among other, blander paving materials. Be sure to bed them in a strong, frost-resistant mortar.

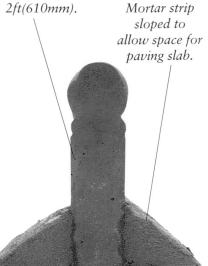

Terracotta rope edging is sold in lengths of about 2ft(610mm).

Mortar strip sloped to allow space for paving slab.

**Above:** *Secure terracotta edging strips in place with a strip of mortar along each side. Slope it as shown and check that it is low enough to allow the paving to butt up against it.*

*1 Set the rope edging and matching corner posts in place. Then spread a bed of sloppy mortar over the area you intend to pave. Place the corner tile first, then add further tiles.*

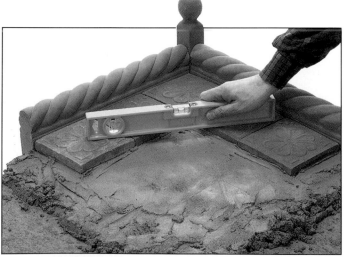

*2 After laying a few tiles along each row, check that the tiles appear level when viewed against the edging. Use a spirit level to ensure that each row is level across the tiled area.*

*3 Here, decorative tiles form a border to plain terracotta pavers, each equivalent in size to four tiles. Place the paver on the mortar bed, tamp it down and check the levels.*

## Cutting pavers

**1** To cut a paver, score a cutting line deeply across its face. Draw the corner of a bolster chisel against a straightedge for accuracy.

**2** Place the paver on a sand bed and cut it with a chisel and hammer. Move the chisel along the line until the paver splits cleanly.

**Left:** Traditional rope edging provides the perfect edging to this dog-leg path, its color contrasting well with the predominantly gray herringbone pattern of the block pavers.

**Below:** Bright blue ceramic tiles add a gaudy flash of color to a brick path inset with pieces of broken paving slab. Outdoor tiles must be frostproof.

Use a strong mortar - 1 part cement to 3 or 4 parts sand, plus added plasticizer - to bed the edging in place.

**4** This completed module shows how the edging, tiles and pavers are coordinated in size. The edging length matches three tile widths, while the paver is equivalent to four tiles in area.

# Pebbles and cobbles

Naturally rounded pebbles and larger cobblestones are a good way of introducing varieties of shape and texture to your paving. You can use them to create paths and patios, but they are more commonly used as a visual counterpoint to flat surfaces - perhaps as a border or to highlight a garden feature, such as a sundial or statue. Their advantage over other garden paving materials is their relatively small size, which makes it easy to fit them round curves and irregularly shaped obstacles. However, because of this, they do take much longer to lay than other materials. You can buy pebbles and cobblestones from builders' suppliers and garden centers, in a range of sizes and colors. Small quantities - enough for an individual garden feature - are usually sold in bags, but for larger areas it will be more economical to buy the stones loose by weight. Ask your supplier for advice about coverage, and have large quantities delivered; more than two or three sacks will wreck your vehicle suspension. It is best to bed the pebbles and cobblestones in mortar, especially if they form a surface that will be walked on or are being used to line a watercourse or surround a fountain, but in decorative areas within flower beds they can be loose-laid. Loose pebbles have a practical use, too; they will discourage weed growth and prevent soil erosion in areas of the garden that are in permanent shade.

1 *You can outline a pebble path with a border of paving bricks or granite setts. Spread a generous mortar bed, set the bricks in place and point neatly between them.*

*Left: Cobblestones set in mortar form a contrasting border to a path of granite setts. Soil will gradually fill the joints and disguise the bedding.*

*Right: Mixing pebbles of different colors can create unusual visual effects. Here, dark pebbles cleverly mimic a narrow meandering stream.*

**2** Start placing the pebbles on the mortar bed, butting them up closely to the border or other feature and to each other. Select individual stones for their fit and the color contrast with their neighbours.

**3** Once you have completed an area of pebbles, use an offcut and a club hammer to tamp them down well into the mortar bed. It is important to ensure that they cannot subsequently work loose.

**Above:** This striking pebble path has been created by placing small, flattish pebbles in a mortar bed, and has a border of small, square paving blocks laid in a gentle curve.

Use bricks, block pavers or stone setts to define the boundaries of a pebble path or other feature.

**5** Water dramatically enhances the natural colors and textures of pebbles. Create this look artificially by coating the finished bed with a clear silicone masonry sealant.

**4** Place a wooden straightedge and spirit level across the surface of the pebbles to check that they are reasonably level. If any project too far above their neighbors, tamp them down further.

# Laying a gravel path

A path or other area of gravel can be an attractive feature in any garden, especially when used to provide contrast alongside flat paving materials. True gravel is just small, water-rounded pebbles, and is available in a range of mixed natural-earth shades that look particularly good when wet. You can also buy crushed stone, which is rough-edged rather than smooth, in colors ranging from white through reds and greens to gray and black. Although both look attractive and are relatively inexpensive to lay, they have several drawbacks from the practical point of view. They need some form of edge restraint, such as curbstones or pegged boards, to stop the stones from migrating onto lawns or into flowerbeds. They need regular raking and weeding to keep them looking good. They can attract the unwanted attentions of dogs and cats, who find them ideal as an earth closet. Lastly, pushing a laden wheelbarrow along a gravel path is akin to the 13th labor of Hercules! However, if you decide that gravel is the surface for you, you will need to work out carefully how much material to order. Decorative aggregates are sold in small carry-home bags, commonly weighing from 55 to 110lbs (25 to 50kg), and by volume in large canvas slings or in loose loads that are delivered to your door. You will need a bulk delivery for all but the smallest areas. A cubic yard of gravel weighs well over a ton, and will cover an area of about 12sq yds to a depth of about 3in(75mm); in metric terms a cubic metre weighs about 1.7 tonnes and will cover just over 13sq m to the same depth.

*3 The best way of discouraging weeds from growing up through a gravel path is to put down a porous membrane (normally used to line plant containers) over the subsoil.*

*1 Excavate the area over which you want to lay the gravel until you reach solid subsoil. Then set out preservative-treated boards around the perimeter of the excavated area and drive in stout corner pegs.*

*2 Secure the boards to the pegs with galvanized nails. Add further pegs at roughly 3ft (about 1m) intervals along the boards all round the area to prevent the boards from bowing outwards later on.*

*5* Compact the layer by running a heavy garden roller over it. Fill in any hollows and roll again until you no longer leave footprints in the surface.

*6* Without disturbing the compacted base layer, spread out the gravel or decorative stone. Fill the area up to the level of the perimeter boards.

*4* To form a firm base for the gravel, cover the membrane with a layer of crushed rock or fine hardcore. You need at least 2in(50mm) of rock on firm subsoil, more if it is soft.

## Mix and match

You can mix smooth paving materials, such as slabs or block pavers, with gravel or crushed stone to create interesting and attractive patterns and contrasts.

*7* Level the gravel with a rake. Draw a wooden straightedge along the tops of the perimeter boards to identify high spots or hollows. Rake again.

**Right:** To use gravel on sloping sites, cut shallow steps into the slope and peg retaining timbers at the front and sides of each one. Add the gravel.

# Gravel gardening

When it comes to giving your garden a soft, natural look, do not underestimate the versatility of gravel. It is one of the most effective ways of reducing work in the garden, acting as an ideal alternative to grass for narrow paths and for informally planted areas, where keeping the grass looking neat can be difficult. It forms a pleasing contrast to low-growing plants and can be used in conjunction with other paving materials on patios and other walkways. Areas of gravel are a particularly popular feature of oriental-style gardens, where the material is used extensively to create unusual dry landscapes adorned with larger stones and styled by raking so that it resembles ripples and waves on water. The effect is extremely restful on the eye and of course the design can be changed at will with a few strokes of the rake. In this context, it is best to use stones of a uniform color, but elsewhere you may want to experiment with the wide range of crushed aggregates available from builders' merchants and garden centers. They are available in colors ranging from glistening white to slate green, sandstone and jet black, and look particularly striking when wet.

*Above:* In oriental-style gardens, fine gravel is raked into soft ripples and waves that contrast with large stones and areas of smaller pebbles. The bamboo screen adds another authentic touch.

*Right:* A simple gravel path is the perfect complement for an informally-planted cottage garden, where the free forms of the planting can tumble unrestrained over the path edge.

**Right:** *Driving short, preservative-treated wooden stakes into the ground in a variety of ornamental patterns restrains the gravel and adds visual contrast to the surface.*

**Below:** *This gravel path meanders its way between neatly trimmed banks of* Heuchera, *a hardy perennial with leaves that remain green all year.*

**Above:** *Gravel does tend to migrate onto lawns and flowerbeds. You can minimize the problem by edging the graveled area with hard paving materials and letting the gravel fill the gaps between the slabs.*

# Wooden decking

Wooden decking is a natural alternative to hard paving in both formal and informal gardens. The raw material is widely available and costs broadly the same as paving (unless you choose an exotic hardwood instead of softwood). It is much easier to cut to size than paving slabs or blocks, quickly blends in with its surroundings as it weathers and is more forgiving to walk or sit down on than hard paving. The only disadvantages of wooden decking are that it will need some occasional maintenance work and that it can be slippery in wet weather. Make sure that all the sawn joists and planed planks for the decking have been pretreated with preservative and apply a preservative stain to the completed structure, paying special attention to any cut ends you have sawn during construction. To keep the decking clear of damp ground and reduce the incidence of rot, set the joists on bricks, ideally with a pad of damp-proof membrane or roofing felt between bricks and joists. Clear the ground beneath the decking and apply a long-term weedkiller before you begin.

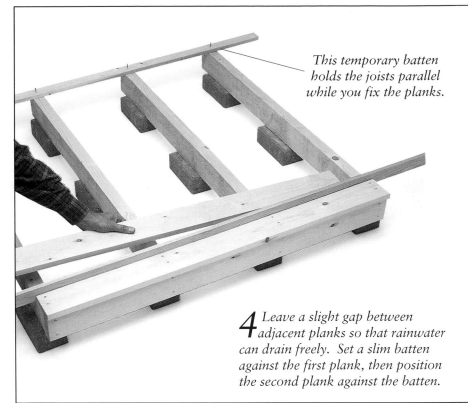

*This temporary batten holds the joists parallel while you fix the planks.*

*4 Leave a slight gap between adjacent planks so that rainwater can drain freely. Set a slim batten against the first plank, then position the second plank against the batten.*

*1 On firm ground, bricks are the simplest way of supporting the joists. Space them evenly, using a plank to align the joist ends and to check that the tops are level.*

*2 Cut a fascia board to match the width of the decking and secure it to the joist ends with galvanized nails. Fix a batten across the tops of the joists at the other end of the decking.*

*3 Cut the first plank to length, position it across the joists so that its front edge projects over the fascia board and forms a projecting nosing. Secure it to each joist with two nails.*

**5** Secure the plank to each joist with two galvanized nails. You can use a string line as a guide to help you align the nail heads across the decking.

**6** The completed decking is an attractive feature in its own right. There is no limit to the size and shape of decking you can create.

*Where decking is used as a sitting area, it is a good idea to add a perimeter batten along the sides and rear of the area to stop chairs being inadvertently pushed off the edge.*

**Above:** Butt-join planks as necessary over the center line of a joist. Sand the cut ends first to prevent splinters.

**Above:** Treat the decking with a preservative stain to improve its resistance to rot and insect attack.

**Above:** Wooden decking can extend to cover as large an area as you need. Here, the planks are laid at an angle to the house wall and a shallow step down to the gravel path below copes with the gentle slope.

Set decking on bricks or blocks bedded in the subsoil so that the joists are held clear of the ground. Hide the supports with pebbles or low-level planting.

# Decking designs

Since wood is easy to cut to size and shape, you can create any number of decorative designs. Carefully work out the design on paper first, adjusting the spacing between the planks to ensure that a whole number will fit the area you want to cover. You can create chevron and diamond patterns by reversing the direction of the planking on adjacent areas of the decking. To protect bare feet in summer, make sure that all cut ends are free from splinters by rounding off cut edges slightly with sandpaper. Provide additional protection for the perimeter of the decking by nailing on edge battens all round. This also helps to reduce water penetration of the vulnerable end grain.

**5** Nail on the first plank. Drive in the nail nearest the corner first, check the alignment of the plank with the pencil lines, and secure it with two more nails.

**6** Use a slim batten as a spacing guide to ensure that the gaps between adjacent boards are the same across the decking surface. Offer up the next plank.

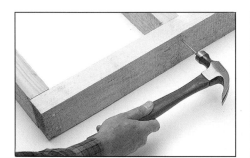

**1** Use preservative-treated sawn softwood for the joists. Space them out evenly and nail a transverse joist to their ends to hold them in position.

**2** To set the planks at a 45° angle to the joists, use a combination square to position the first plank at the corner of the joist framework.

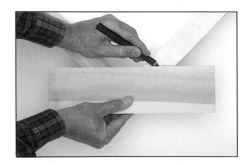

**3** Once you have positioned the first plank accurately, remove the square and mark the plank position on the joists below with a pencil.

**4** Use the square, again with its 45° face against the edge of the plank, to mark a guideline for the nails above the center line of the joist beneath.

**7** Repeat the procedure with the square and pencil to ensure that the nails securing the second plank are in line with those holding the first one.

A combination square (or adjustable try square) is an excellent tool for checking and marking angles.

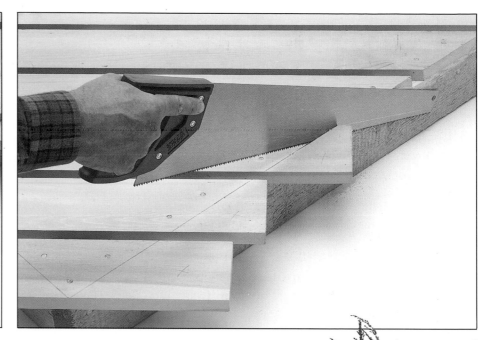

*8* Use the spacer batten to position subsequent planks, nailing them to the joists one by one. Punch the nail heads just below the surface of the wood for a safe and attractive finish.

*9* When all the planks are nailed to the joists, place a straightedge over the projecting ends, align it with the outer face of the joist below and mark a cutting line across each plank.

*10* Use a panel saw to cut off the projecting ends of the planks. Saw just on the waste side of the cutting line, taking care to keep the saw blade vertical as you work.

*11* Sand all the cut ends of the planks to remove any splinters. Then nail on edging battens to give the decking area a neat finish. This will also help to protect the exposed end grain against rot and damage.

*12* You can treat the finished decking with clear wood preservative (as here), a colored preservative stain or wood dye. Avoid varnish, which will soon blister and crack.

# Garden decks

Wood is a material that allows your inventiveness full rein when it comes to creating walkways and sitting areas in the garden. Unlike masonry, it is light and easy to handle, and can be worked with simple and familiar tools, allowing you to use it on any scale and in any way you wish. Set alongside a garden pond or other water feature, it conjures up images of sturdy wooden jetties on a boating lake. Placed amongst an overflowing border, it creates a natural-looking pathway that blends in with the informality of the planting far more sympathetically than any masonry path can. The structures you create with it can be built *in situ* on a grand scale, or can be assembled from small modules put together in your workshop and then arranged - and rearranged at will - in the garden. However you decide to use it, remember the two essential rules. Firstly, all wood that spends its life in contact with the ground must either be a naturally durable species, or else be thoroughly pretreated with wood preservative to keep rot and insect attack at bay. Secondly, wood can become slippery when wet since moss and algae will grow on its surface, so be prepared to scrub it down once or twice a year to keep it in a safe condition and looking good.

*Right: This semi-circular wooden deck was created using sheets of exterior-grade plywood. The grooves radiate from the center of the water feature and were cut using a power router.*

*Left: Prefabricated, preservative-treated square decking panels with a non-slip grooved surface pattern can be laid directly on the soil and provide the perfect complement for an informal border of ferns, hostas and ivy.*

**Above:** *You can cut any sturdy, second-hand structural woodwork, such as old floor joists, into short lengths and use them to form a garden path. Soak them in wood preservative first, however.*

**Left:** *A tailor-made wooden walkway over a garden pond makes the perfect vantage point for watching the fish. Its supporting framework rests on masonry piers built within the pond itself.*

# Decking tiles

You can buy small, preassembled wooden decking tiles made from preservative-treated softwood. Simply lay these on supporting joists to create whatever area of decking you require.

**Below:** *Decking tiles have closely spaced slats held together by two stapled-on support battens.*

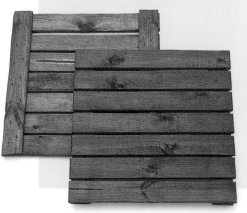

**1** Make up a framework of preservative-treated joists to support the tiles. Space the joists to allow the tiles to meet along the center line of each joist and lay in the individual tiles.

**2** Nail the tiles through the slats into the joists beneath. If you prefer to make invisible fixings, place screws in the gaps between the slats and drive them through the support battens.

'Traditional' planked decking.

**3** In this case, all the tiles have been laid with their slats running in the same direction.

**Left:** *For a checker-board effect, rotate alternate tiles through 90°. Or lay adjacent rows of tiles with the slats in one row at right angles to those in the next row.*

# Building a brick wall

Most gardeners choose bricks for outdoor building projects. Bricks are relatively inexpensive, widely available and supplied in standard sizes and in a wide range of colors and textures. This makes it easy to create garden features to match the house masonry or, alternatively, to bring some contrast into the garden by using a radically different color scheme. Apart from choosing a brick for its looks, there are two other important factors to consider: its quality and its type. Bricks used in the garden must obviously be weatherproof, so check that you buy at least ordinary quality bricks or, better still, special quality. The former are durable enough for most jobs but will not withstand severe exposure to the weather, so do not use them for the top course of a free-standing wall or for building earth-retaining walls. As far as brick type is concerned, the choice lies between *commons* and *facing* bricks. You can use so-called commons wherever the appearance of the brickwork does not matter, but facings are the better choice for projects where looks are as important as performance.

*2 Use a mortar mix of 1 part cement, 1 part lime or liquid plasticizer and 5 parts building sand. Spread a generous bed of mortar on the foundation strip.*

*1 Most garden brickwork will involve turning corners. Draw the building line on the foundation strip in chalk and use a square to mark a perfect right angle at each corner.*

*The concrete foundation should be at least twice as wide as the wall.*

*3 Set the first brick on the mortar bed. Tamp it down with the handle of a club hammer and check that the brick is level in both directions.*

*4 Butter a generous wedge of mortar onto the end of the next and each subsequent brick before putting it in place. This will abut the brick that is already in position and forms the vertical mortar joint between bricks.*

**5** To turn a corner in stretcher-bond brickwork - bricks laid end to end - place the next brick at right angles to the first one and tamp it down so it is level with and square to its neighbor.

*Pegged string lines are helpful positional guides when setting out the first course of bricks, but have been omitted here for clarity.*

**6** Continue adding bricks end to end to complete the first course. Start the second course with a corner brick placed vertically above the corner brick in the course below.

**7** Complete the second course. Repeat the layout in the first two courses to build up the wall. Check the levels as you work with a spirit level and straightedge laid across the wall.

## Making a set square

A builder's square helps to set out right angled corners accurately. The simplest way of making one is to cut a triangle off the corner of an offcut of plywood. The bigger the square the more accurate it will be, but keep it to a manageable size for ease of handling.

*Scoop up mortar droppings from the foundation strip.*

*Trim excess mortar from the joints as you work; you can point them later.*

41

# Building a brick wall

Laying bricks is very satisfying and not difficult to master if you put in a little practice. Apart from getting used to handling mortar confidently, the most important skill is keeping the bricks evenly spaced and square with each other throughout the wall structure. A spirit level is an invaluable aid at every stage to check that each course of bricks is laid truly level - both along the wall and across its thickness - and to ensure that the face of the wall is truly vertical. If any errors go undetected, they can quickly throw the whole wall structure out of line. The easiest way to keep the thickness of the horizontal joints constant is with a homemade gauge rod marked with brick and joint heights; hold it vertically against the face of the wall after bedding each course in place. It can also be used to check that all the brick faces are in line. To keep vertical joints evenly spaced, use the technique of racking back: building up wall ends and corners as steps. Then use a straightedge held parallel to the slope to check that all the brick edges are in line and, therefore, that the joints are of even thickness. When you have built the ends and corners up to the final wall height in this way, simply fill in the remaining bricks in each course using those already laid as a guide to line and level. Trim off excess mortar from the joints and point them neatly.

*1 As the wall rises, use a gauge rod held vertically against the wall face to check that all the horizontal mortar joints are the same thickness.*

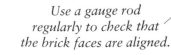

*2 Start each new course of brickwork by placing and leveling the corner, or end, brick. Check that the brick is facing the right way to maintain the bonding arrangement in each course.*

## Making a gauge rod

*Professional bricklayers are adept at laying bricks with a constant joint thickness, but this is harder for the amateur. A simple gauge rod is a big help in ensuring even joints.*

*1 Set out a row of bricks on their faces, ⅜in(10mm) apart. Hold a length of planed wood on top of the bricks and mark all the joint positions.*

*2 Extend the pencil marks across the face of the gauge and onto one edge. Allow for a mortar joint at ground level.*

*Use a gauge rod regularly to check that the brick faces are aligned.*

**3** As you place each brick and tamp it down into its mortar bed, use the edge of your trowel to trim off excess mortar from the joint on both faces of the wall. Scoop up the mortar droppings to keep the site tidy.

Hold the trowel with its blade flat to the wall as you trim off the mortar.

**4** After completing between four and six courses, point the joints before the mortar can harden off. Use a pointing trowel to form a sloping weathered joint.

**Above:** Use a straightedge to check that the racking back at ends and corners is even, evidence that the vertical joints are all of the same thickness.

At the end of the wall, each alternate course will finish with a half-brick.

**5** The completed corner resembles a stepped pyramid. Build up the other corner or end of the wall in the same way. Complete each course in turn using end bricks - plus a string line if you wish - as a guide.

Remember to finish the bottom joint neatly, too.

Brickwork gets its strength from the way the bricks in each course interlock, a process known as bonding. The simplest bricklaying bond, stretcher bond, is used in walls 4in(100mm) thick, and is created by offsetting the bricks in each course by half their length. Alternate courses end with a cut half-brick, unless the wall turns a corner, in which case the end brick in alternate courses is laid at 90° to the others to start the next section of the wall. Such a wall is not very strong, however, and should not be more than about 21in(530mm) or seven bricks high unless reinforcing piers are incorporated to strengthen the structure (see page 46). For walls higher than this you should use brickwork 8½in(215mm) thick, and there are several established alternative methods of arranging the bonding in walls built in this way. In theory, you could simply build up the wall as two 'leaves' of stretcher-bond brickwork, relying on the strength of the mortar between them to hold the wall together, but this does not create a particularly strong wall unless you incorporate metal ties to bond the two leaves together. Instead, you need to lay some of the bricks end-on as headers so that they pass right through the wall and bond the whole structure together. You can build a free-standing wall in this way to a height of 4ft 9in (1.45m) or 19 bricks without piers, and to 6ft(1.8m) or 24 bricks if the wall has piers at roughly 10ft(3m) centers. The result is a strong and stable wall, with attractive patterns in the brickwork as the courses are built up.

**ENGLISH WALL BOND**
*This walling bond has alternate courses laid in running (stretcher) bond and header bond; in other words, one course with the bricks laid face out, followed by a course laid with the brick ends exposed.*

*Stretcher bond*

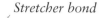

**ENGLISH BOND - LAYER A**
*If the wall turns a corner, lay one section in stretcher bond and the return section in header bond. A queen closer - a brick cut in half along its length - is included in the header course next to the corner brick to maintain the bonding pattern.*

*Queen closer. Alternatively, use two quarter-bricks.*

*Header bond*

**ENGLISH BOND - LAYER B**
*The second course is a perfect mirror image of the first, with stretchers laid over the first-course headers and vice versa. Again, use a queen closer at the corner, but lay it at right angles to the one in the course below.*

**Right:** *As the wall builds up, the appearance of the alternating stretchers and headers becomes clear. The queen closer next to the corner stretcher maintains the bonding arrangement in successive courses.*

*Cut queen closers with an angle grinder if you have one. Otherwise, use two cut quarter-bricks laid end to end.*

## FLEMISH WALL BOND

*In this walling bond, each course is built up by repeating the use of a pair of bricks laid in stretcher bond, followed by a single header brick passing right through the wall to tie the structure together.*

### FLEMISH BOND - LAYER A

*If the wall turns a corner, lay each course using the same arrangement of stretchers and headers. Incorporate a queen closer next to the corner header to maintain the bonding arrangement in successive courses.*

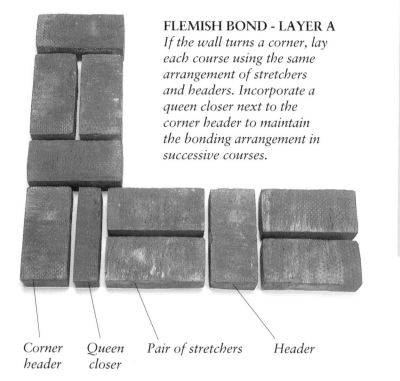

Corner header | Queen closer | Pair of stretchers | Header

### FLEMISH BOND -LAYER B

*In the second course, reverse the corner header first and place a queen closer next to it. Then lay alternate header bricks and pairs of stretchers along each section of the wall.*

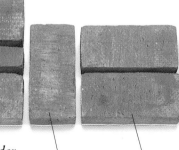

Corner header reversed with queen closer next to it. | Header | Pair of stretchers

*Right: This attractive corner planter is built with two leaves of stretcher-bond brickwork topped with two layers of quarry tiles and a capping course of bricks laid on edge.*

## How many bricks will I need?

*When it comes to estimating the number of bricks you will need to build a wall, use these figures as a guide: 50 bricks per sq yd (60 per sq m) of wall built in stretcher bond; 100 per sq yd (120 per sq m) for bonds such as English and Flemish where the fished wall is one brick thick. Add an extra five per cent to your quantities for breakages.*

*The pleasing symmetry of Flemish bond is revealed as the wall builds up in height, with each course showing alternate headers and stretchers on each face of the wall.*

# Building brick piers

When you are building free-standing walls, you must ensure that the structure is strong enough to withstand lateral forces - strong winds and accidental impacts in particular. You can do this up to a point by increasing the wall thickness; a wall one brick thick will obviously be stronger than one only half a brick thick, and a one-and-a-half brick wall will be stronger still. The maximum heights to which you can safely build walls in these three thicknesses are respectively 21in(530mm) or seven bricks, 4ft 9in(1.45m) or 19 bricks, and 8ft(2.44m) or 32 bricks, and you should reduce the height if you live in a very exposed area. However, it is often not economical to increase the wall thickness along its entire length. Instead, the strategy is to incorporate piers at intervals to provide the necessary reinforcement. These are generally twice the wall thickness, and are used at the ends of the wall, at corners and at intervals of about 10ft(3m) along the length of the wall. With a half-brick wall, piers one brick square are built so as to be visible on only one side of the wall. Alternatively, piers one-and-a-half bricks square can be used; in this case, the piers are visible from both sides of the wall.

## BUILDING AN END PIER

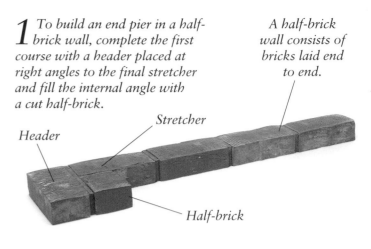

**1** To build an end pier in a half-brick wall, complete the first course with a header placed at right angles to the final stretcher and fill the internal angle with a cut half-brick.

A half-brick wall consists of bricks laid end to end.

*Header*

*Stretcher*

*Half-brick*

**2** In the second course, lay two stretchers on the pier and carry on the course with more stretchers laid along the wall.

*Two stretchers to form the second layer of the pier.*

## Cutting bricks

If you need to cut a brick to size, start by marking the cutting line on the brick and score it all round with the tip of a brick bolster, bricklayer's chisel. Place the brick on a bed of sand and drive the chisel with blows from a club hammer to break the brick at the marked cutting position.

*Make sure that all the internal joints in the pier are filled with mortar.*

*Build up the wall with a stepped arrangement and fill in each course when the end piers are completed.*

**3** Repeat the bonding arrangements for the first two courses to build up the pier and the wall to the required height.

*Viewed from the reverse angle, the pier structure is identical to that of an external corner in stretcher-bond brickwork.*

## BUILDING AN INTERMEDIATE PIER

*1* To build an intermediate pier in a half-brick wall, place two headers side by side at the pier position. You need piers at roughly 10ft(3m) intervals along the length of the wall.

Headers

*2* In the second course, center a half-brick over the headers at the pier position and flank it with two three-quarter bricks to maintain the bonding arrangement on the face of the wall.

Half-brick    Threequarter brick

Threequarter brick

Complete the pier with a whole brick.

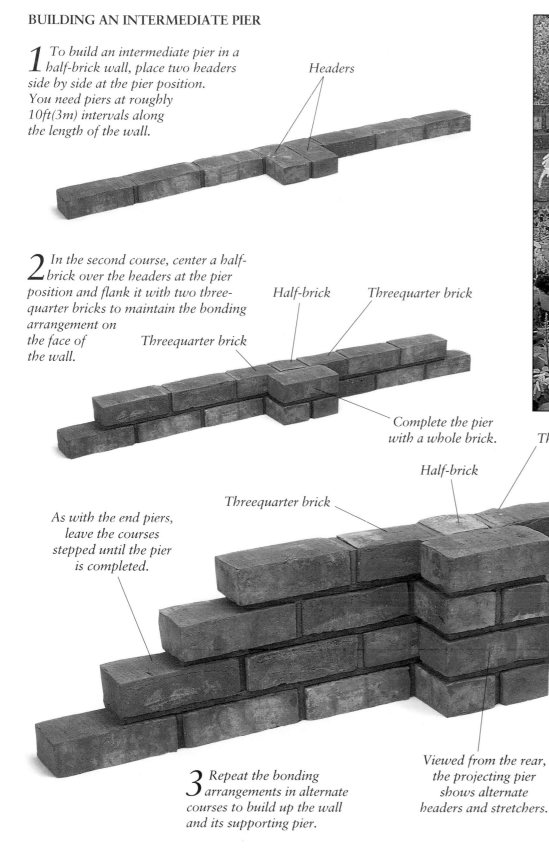

As with the end piers, leave the courses stepped until the pier is completed.

Threequarter brick

Half-brick

Threequarter brick

**Above:** *Each course of this pier contains three bricks. In the first course, two bricks are laid side by side and the third is laid at right angles to their ends. The arrangement is reversed in alternate courses.*

*3* Repeat the bonding arrangements in alternate courses to build up the wall and its supporting pier.

Viewed from the rear, the projecting pier shows alternate headers and stretchers.

**Right:** *Viewed from the face of the wall, the symmetry of the brick bonding in alternate courses is clearly visible as the wall rises. Check that the joints are aligned vertically.*

# A stone block wall

**2** *After completing the first course of the wall, neaten the vertical joints between the blocks and spread a bed of mortar on top of them, ready for the second course.*

Compared with the regular appearance of most garden brickwork, stone walls have a pleasing informality. You can build them in natural stone if you have a good local source of supply, but it takes considerable skill to bond irregularly shaped blocks into a sound structure. Man-made garden walling blocks, on the other hand, offer the best of all worlds. They show the same attractive face to the world as natural stone, but have flat tops and bottoms so that they can be laid and bonded easily, just like bricks. They are much easier to cut if necessary, using ordinary masonry tools. Above all, they are readily available from all the usual suppliers. The blocks are made from reconstituted stone - fine aggregates bonded together with mortar and hydraulically pressed to give them strength. They are available in colors ranging from shades of gray to reds, buffs and yellows. Block sizes vary, but the commonest measures about 9in(230mm) long, 4in(100mm) wide and 2½in(65mm) high. Some ranges include longer and thicker blocks, allowing you to build walls with irregular coursing as if using natural stone. You can leave the top course of the wall exposed, but since its surface usually has a visible mold mark it will look more attractive if you finish it with a row of matching coping stones. These are commonly 24in (610mm) long and have a slightly ridged upper surface and drip grooves along their undersides, features designed to help rainwater to run off and fall clear of the wall face below. The colors match the walling blocks. You can easily cut them down to complete a run of coping, using the same tools as for cutting the walling blocks.

**1** *Lay a suitable foundation - a strip or slab of concrete about 6in(150mm) thick and at least twice as wide as the wall thickness. Spread a mortar bed along the building line and bed the first course in place.*

*Blocks have one textured face and end. Check as you work that you lay them the correct way round.*

*Use a mortar mix of 1 part cement, 1 part lime and 5 parts building sand.*

48

**3** To maintain the bonding pattern in the second course, place a half-block at one end of the wall. Cut it with a bricklayer's chisel and hammer.

**4** After laying two or three whole blocks, use a spirit level to check that they are horizontal both along the wall direction and at right angles to it.

**5** Butter some mortar onto the end of each block before butting it up against the previous block to leave a vertical joint about ⅜in(10mm) thick.

**6** When you have built up the wall to the height you want, spread mortar on top of the final course of blocks and lay the coping stones in place.

Position the coping stones so that they overlap the wall faces and ends by the same amount all round.

**7** Trim off excess mortar from all the joints and neaten them with the tip of your pointing trowel. Alternatively, recess them using an offcut of garden hose.

The foundation should be 6in(150mm) thick and twice as wide as the wall.

# Building a screen wall

By their very nature, brick and stone walls provide a solid structure that is ideal for boundary walls. However, there may be situations where you would prefer an open screen, perhaps to surround a patio without cutting out too much sunlight or to conceal an eyesore. Pierced screen walling blocks are one option. These square blocks are easy to build up into a see-through screen that you can either leave to weather naturally or decorate with masonry paint. The blocks are a standard 11⅜in(290mm) square, so they build up into a regular 11¾in (300mm) grid with a ⅜in(10mm) thick mortar joint and are usually 3⅝in(90mm) thick. Since they cannot be cut down in size, any wall you build with them must be an exact multiple of 11¾in(300mm) in length and height. You can use the blocks on their own to create a complete screen, building up end, corner and intermediate piers with specially shaped pilaster blocks that are sized so that three match the height of two walling blocks. As an alternative, you can build areas of blockwork into solid brick or stone walls as decorative infill panels. As the blocks are simply stack-bonded in vertical columns instead of having an interlocking bond like brickwork, a wall more than about two courses high is inherently very weak and could be toppled by high winds.

**1** *Spread a bed of mortar along the building line on your foundation strip and draw the tip of your trowel along it to create a series of ridges.*

**2** *To build a free-standing wall, set the first pilaster block in place on the mortar bed. The end pier block shown here has one recessed face.*

**3** *Set a spirit level on top of the block to check that it is level in both directions. If necessary, tamp it down with the handle of a club hammer.*

*Remember that screen walling blocks are relatively fragile. When tamping them down into the mortar bed, strike them close to the corner so that the force of the blow is transmitted downwards through solid material.*

**4** *Butter some mortar onto one edge of the first walling block, rest it on the mortar bed and lower it into position so that it fits into the recess in the pilaster block.*

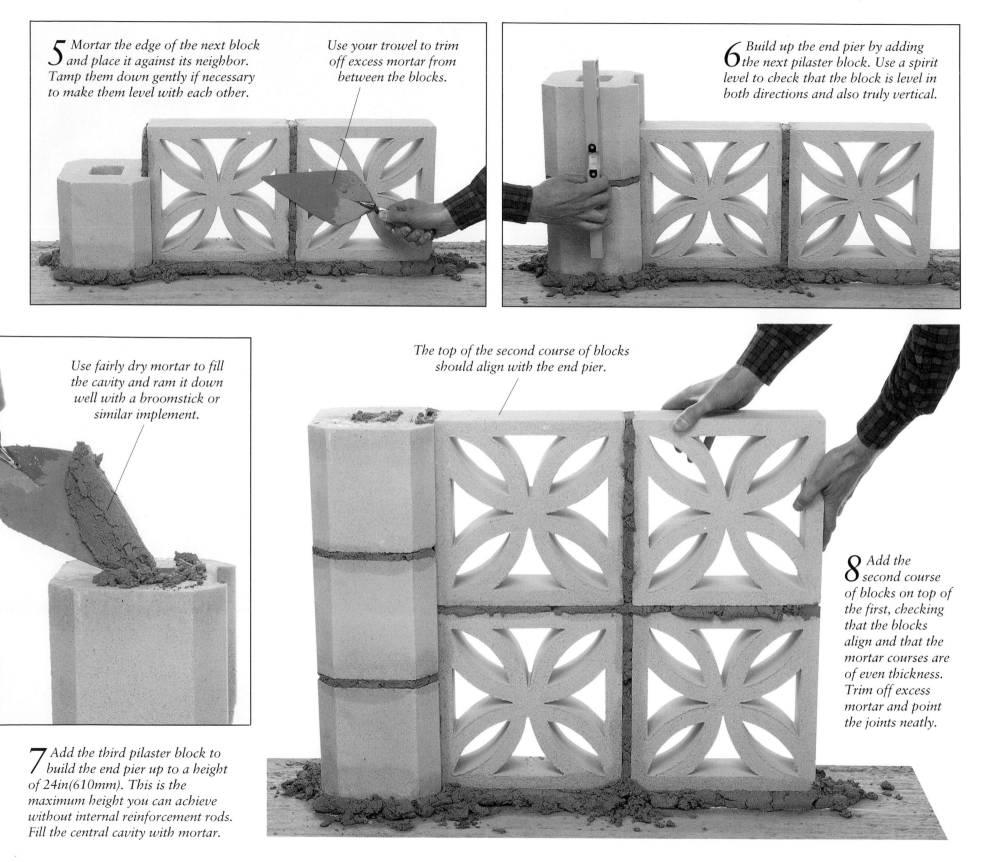

**5** Mortar the edge of the next block and place it against its neighbor. Tamp them down gently if necessary to make them level with each other.

Use your trowel to trim off excess mortar from between the blocks.

**6** Build up the end pier by adding the next pilaster block. Use a spirit level to check that the block is level in both directions and also truly vertical.

Use fairly dry mortar to fill the cavity and ram it down well with a broomstick or similar implement.

The top of the second course of blocks should align with the end pier.

**7** Add the third pilaster block to build the end pier up to a height of 24in(610mm). This is the maximum height you can achieve without internal reinforcement rods. Fill the central cavity with mortar.

**8** Add the second course of blocks on top of the first, checking that the blocks align and that the mortar courses are of even thickness. Trim off excess mortar and point the joints neatly.

# Building a screen wall

**1** If the wall is rising no higher than two courses, it needs no additional reinforcement. Simply spread a layer of mortar on top of the wall and pier blocks, ready for the pier caps and coping stones.

*Right:* The makers of screen walling supply special pilaster blocks that you can use to build corners, intermediate piers and three-way piers where one wall meets another at right angles. All these blocks are 8in(200mm) high.

This block is used to form a corner pier where two walls meet at right angles.

This block is used to form intermediate piers at 10ft(3m) intervals on long walls.

**2** Set the pier cap in place first, checking that it is centered on the pier blocks. Then position the first length of coping, butting it up to the pier cap. Tamp it down gently so that it is perfectly level.

**3** Use your pointing trowel to finish off the joints between the blocks. You can either add a little more mortar to create flush pointing, or draw the trowel along each joint to produce a sloping weathered joint.

This block is used to form a three-way pier where another wall meets the first one at right angles.

## Building higher

To strengthen a taller wall structure - more than two courses of walling blocks high - build the piers around reinforcing rods set in the foundations, as shown here. The wall can be completed with pier caps and coping stones that match the color and finish of the screen walling blocks.

**1** Bond every other course of blocks to the piers with a strip of expanded metal mesh.

**2** Hook the mesh strip over the reinforcing rod, press it down into the mortar bed and add a little more mortar on top of it before positioning the next course.

**4** This walling module shows how two wall blocks exactly match the height of three pier blocks. Any wall with pier blocks must therefore have an even number of courses.

**3** Lift the next pier block over the top of the reinforcing rod and lower it into position. As you place it, make sure that the slot in which the wall blocks locate is facing the correct way.

**4** Add two more courses of walling blocks and two more pier blocks. If the wall will be more than four courses high, allow the mortar to harden overnight before continuing as before.

# Putting up fence posts

Whatever type of fencing you erect, you must ensure that the supporting posts are secure. The traditional way of doing this is to bury part of the post in the ground and anchor it in place with a collar of concrete. The main drawback of this method is that because the base of the post is below ground level, it will eventually rot, even if the wood was treated with preservative. On the other hand, a steel fence spike (and its close relative, the bolt-down fence support designed for use on hard-surfaced areas) keeps the vulnerable post completely above ground level. Both types have a square socket into which you fit the post end and come in sizes to accept 2in(50mm), 3in(75mm) and 4in(100mm) posts. Some have a socket with steel teeth that lock the post permanently in place as it is hammered in. Others have a bolt-operated clamping action reinforced by screws or nails. This system allows you to remove the post without disturbing the socket. Fence spikes are hammered into the ground, using a removable wood or resin striking block to protect the socket from the hammer blows. The most difficult thing is ensuring that the spike remains vertical as it is driven in; underground stones can deflect it, making this type of fixing unsuitable for rocky soils. In this situation, use a shorter spike designed for concreting in. To secure fence supports to concrete or other solid masonry bases, use expanding metal anchors, which allow the support to be removed if necessary in the future.

## Using a fence spike

Choose the spike size to match that of the post you are installing. Buy a special striking block (sometimes called a dolly) to protect the metal socket from the hammer blows.

Sledge hammer

Striking block (dolly)

Fence spike with toothed socket

Use a spirit level (and a post offcut) to check that the spike is being driven in vertically.

Fence spike with clamp socket

*1* *To secure a bolt-down fence support, place it on the surface where it is to stand and mark the positions of the corner fixing holes.*

*2* *Select a masonry drill bit to match the diameter of the expanding anchor you are using and drill out each fixing hole to the required depth.*

*3* *Separate the bolt and washer from the anchor sleeve and push the sleeve into the fixing hole with the expanding plug at the bottom.*

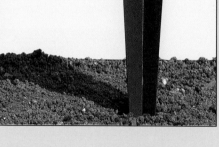

*1* Push the spike into the ground by hand at the required post position. Place the striking block in the socket and start to hammer in the spike.

*2* Regularly check that the spike is being driven in precisely vertically, by holding a spirit level against two adjacent faces of the socket in turn.

*3* Continue to drive the spike in with repeated hammer blows until the base of the socket is at ground level. Then hammer the post into the socket.

*4* Use your spirit level again to check that the post is vertical. If it is not, try tapping the socket sideways to correct the lean.

Check that the support is standing level on the surface.

*4* Stand the fence support in position over the fixing holes and drop in the four bolts. If the support is not truly level, place packing beneath it.

*5* Tighten each bolt firmly. This will expand the anchor fully to ensure a secure fixing in the masonry foundation.

## Clamp-type sockets

Position the post and tighten the bolts as shown here. Drive screws or nails into the post through the holes in the sockets.

# Installing a fence panel

The quickest way of creating a fence that combines privacy and shelter is to erect prefabricated fence panels between the posts. These preservative-treated panels are made from thin wooden strips secured to a lightweight framework, and are available in a variety of styles, in standard 6ft(1.8m) lengths and in heights from 3 to 6ft (915mm to 1.8m). The strips usually run horizontally, and either overlap like shiplap siding or cladding, or are interwoven around vertical battens. The panels are not intrinsically very strong; the completed fence relies for its rigidity on secure fixings, without which high winds can tear the panels away from their supporting posts. A good method is to attach special metal fixing clips to the posts before the panels are set in place between them. Since panels are a standard size and few fencing runs consist of an exact number of whole panels, you will have to cut one or more panels down in width. Lever off the vertical framing battens at one end of the panel and fix them back at the required distance away from the opposite edge to give the panel width you want. Then saw off the unwanted section of the panel, using the repositioned framing batten as a cutting guide. Apply a coat of wood preservative to the panels and posts every two years.

*1 Position the first post using a fence spike or a concrete collar. Check that the post is truly vertical by holding a spirit level against two adjacent faces of the post.*

*2 Nail or screw U-shaped metal fixing clips to the inner face of the post. Use two clips, near the top and bottom, for low panels and add a third clip halfway up for full-height panels.*

*3 Support the fence panel on bricks or offcuts of wood so that the bottom is clear of the ground. Slide the edge of the panel into place against the post. The clips will hold it upright.*

*4 Secure the clip to the panel with galvanized or other rustproof nails. If you have access to the other face of the fence, drive in another nail through the clip from that side, too.*

*5 Site the next post close to the first panel. Allow clearance for the clips. The fence spike should be vertical and on line as you drive it in.*

## Other fixings

L-shaped brackets screw into the post and are themselves screwed to the panel - arguably a stronger fixing than nails, especially in windy areas. If your panels have sturdy perimeter frames, you can drive nails or screws through them into the posts.

**1** Drill a pilot hole. Grip the bracket with pliers and wind the screw into the post, finishing up with the flange on your side.

**2** Support the panel on blocks and use a bradawl to make pilot holes for rustproof screws that will not stain the fence. Drive in the screws.

**Above:** If the framing battens are strong, drill clearance holes to prevent splitting and drive galvanized nails through the battens into the posts.

**6** Attach the fence clips to the second post so that they are at the same level as on the first one. Stand the post in its socket and hammer or clamp it into place. Nail through the fixing clips as before.

**7** Continue adding panels and posts until you reach the end of the fencing run. Fit a cut-to-size panel here if necessary. Nail a cap onto the top of each post.

**8** Remove the support blocks after fixing each panel in place. Keep soil away from the base of the panels to prevent them from rotting.

# A close-boarded fence

The traditional close-boarded fence is one of the strongest and most attractive types of fence you can build, but it contains a lot of solid wood, so it is more expensive than other types. It consists of two or three horizontal rails - called arris rails - to which you nail overlapping vertical boards. You need only two rails for fences up to about 4ft(1.2m) high, and three equally spaced rails for taller fences. Arris rails have a right-angled triangular cross-section and are fitted between the posts with the widest face vertical. In traditional construction, the ends of the rails were tapered and fitted into mortises cut in the fence posts. Nowadays, special metal brackets are usually used to attach the rails to the post faces. The vertical fence boards - known as feather-edge boards - are tapered in cross-section and are fixed to the rail so that the thick edge of one board overlaps the thin edge of its neighbor. Because the vulnerable end-grain of the feather-edge boards is exposed at the top and bottom, it needs some protection from water penetration and rot.

*1 Start by erecting all the posts, spacing them out evenly along the run. Then nail 6in(150mm) lengths of 1in(25mm) square batten to the posts.*

*2 Cut the gravel board to length and brush some wood preservative onto the cut ends. Then set it in place between the posts. A gravel board protects the bottom of the feather-edge boards.*

*On sloping ground, fit the gravel board so that it follows the angle of the slope.*

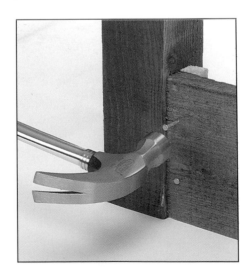

*3 Secure each end of the gravel board to its support block with two galvanized nails. Check that the board is horizontal on level ground.*

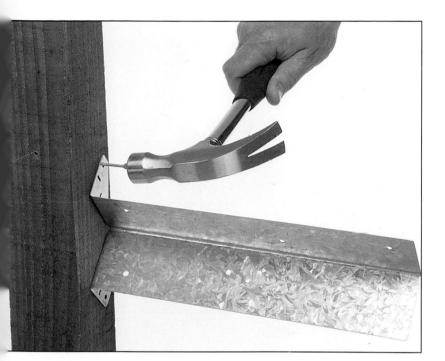

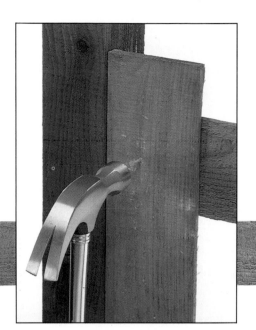

**4** Nail the bottom arris rail bracket about 6in(150mm) up from the top of the gravel board. Nail the second bracket about 6in(150mm) below the top of the fence.

**6** Stand a length of feather-edged board on the gravel board next to one of the posts and mark on it the finished fence height required.

**7** Cut the board to length and treat the cut end with preservative. Use this board on level ground as a template for cutting the rest to length. Stand the first cut-to-length feather-edge board on the gravel board with its thicker edge next to the post. Nail it to each arris rail in turn.

**5** Cut each rail to length and hold it in the jaws of the bracket so you can drive galvanized nails into it through the predrilled fixing holes.

Two arris rails are enough for a fence up to 4ft(1.2m). Add a third rail for taller fences.

# A close-boarded fence

There are two ways of protecting the feather-edge boards from water penetration and rot. One is to fix a capping rail along the top of the fence and the other is to rest the boards on a horizontal length of wood known as a gravel board. This is fixed at ground level to small wooden support blocks nailed to the post sides, and is simple and inexpensive to replace if it becomes rotten as time goes by. When buying materials for making a close-boarded fence, make sure that all the wood has been pretreated with wood preservative, and buy a small quantity of a suitable preservative so that you can treat the ends of any wood you cut to length yourself. If you are building this type of fence as a tall boundary fence, you should construct it with the rails on your side of the boundary so that they cannot be used as an aid to climbing the fence. You may need access to your neighbor's property to build the fence in this way; if you do, always ask permission first.

## Using a nail guide

*If you do not trust your ability to align the nail heads by eye, you can pin a length of string between adjacent posts and use this as a nailing guide. This also ensures that the nails go into the center of the arris rail.*

**1** *Subsequent boards should overlap by about ½in(12mm). Use a wood offcut as a guide to help you keep the overlap constant along the fence.*

**2** *Having set the overlap and checked that the top of the board is level with its neighbor, nail it to the center of the top arris rail.*

**3** *Use a spirit level to check that the board is truly vertical, then nail it to the other arris rail(s). Align the nails horizontally for neatness.*

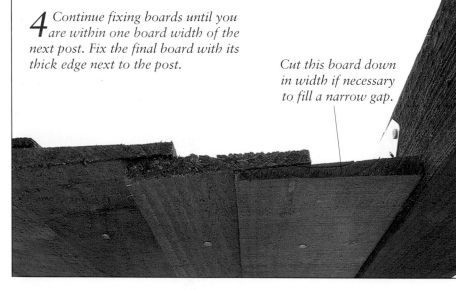

**4** Continue fixing boards until you are within one board width of the next post. Fix the final board with its thick edge next to the post.

Cut this board down in width if necessary to fill a narrow gap.

**5** Cut a length of capping rail to fit between the posts, and nail it to the top of the fence boards. Then fit a cap to each post with two nails.

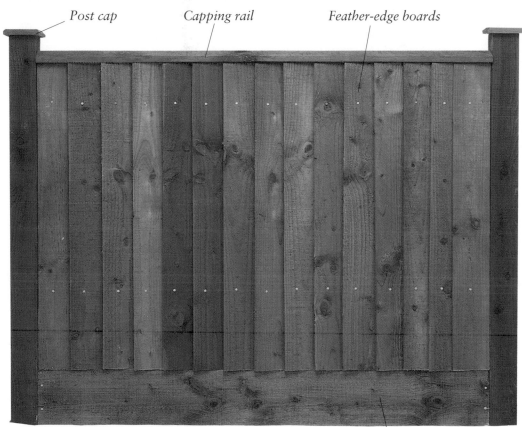

Post cap     Capping rail     Feather-edge boards

**6** The completed fence presents an attractive face to the outside wall. Having the arris rails on your side makes the fence difficult to climb.

Gravel board

**Below:** A traditional close-boarded boundary fence makes the perfect backdrop for any border. It can be topped with trellis panels to encourage climbing plants to clothe the structure.

# A ranch-style fence

This type of fencing, as its name implies, originated on cattle ranches, where its simple construction was sufficient to keep stock securely penned in at minimal cost. It consists of widely spaced horizontal rails fixed to sturdy posts, and is often used as an inexpensive alternative to picket fencing around front gardens, where marking the boundary line is more important than having a high degree of privacy or security. On low fences, two rails are usually sufficient, but three or more can be used on higher fences. Ranch-style fences are seldom built more than about 4ft(1.2m) high, since the extra height would not improve either their looks or their security and would increase the cost of the materials unnecessarily. They are often painted white, but if you want a less visually intrusive fence you can use natural shades of green or brown instead. Whatever color you choose, you can substantially reduce the need for regular redecoration by using a microporous paint or stain. You can improve the security of a ranch-style fence - say, to keep pets in - by fitting an extra rail just above ground level and then stapling on unobtrusive wire mesh between the rails and posts. If you want more privacy and shelter from the prevailing winds than an open ranch-style fence can provide, simply space the rails more closely and fix them alternately to the front and back of the posts so that they present an apparently solid barrier when viewed from a distance. This type of fencing is known as interference, or interlap, fencing. However, it is comparatively expensive in material terms, and is useless as far as security is concerned since it is as easy to climb as a ladder. Restrict its use to screens within the garden, rather than as a boundary fence.

*Above: Cutting the post tops to a 45° angle helps rainwater to run off and reduces the risk of rotting. If you prefer square post tops, fit post caps.*

*Apply a microporous paint or stain. Traditional paints and varnishes soon crack and peel off.*

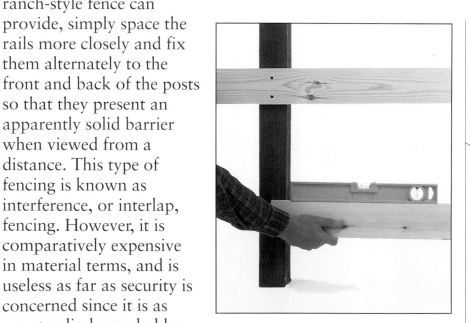

*Above: On level ground, fix one end of each rail at the correct level with a single nail or screw. When the rail is horizontal, drive in the other fixings.*

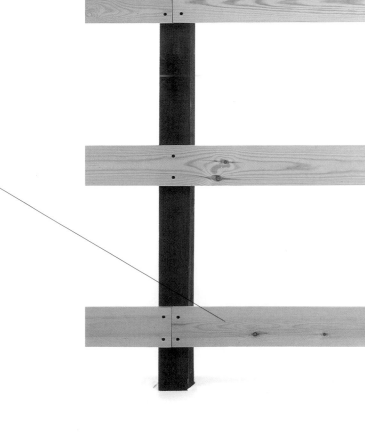

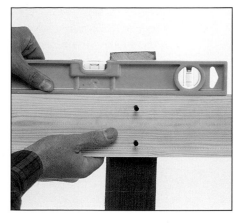

**Above:** *Fix long rails so that they run across the posts. Part-drive the fixings into the rail and, on level ground, check that the rail is horizontal.*

**Above:** *Drive the fixings fully home to secure the rail to the post. Screws are better than nails, which can be pulled out by heavy impacts or vandalism.*

*The two rail ends should butt up tightly against each other.*

**Above:** *The cut rail ends should reach to the center line of the posts. Drill clearance holes to avoid splitting the wood close to the ends.*

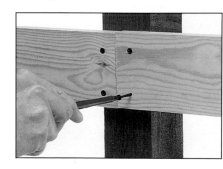

**Above:** *Offer up the next length of rail so that it is aligned with the end of the first one. Drill clearance holes as before and secure the rail.*

## Interference fencing

*Interference, or interlap, fencing consists of closely spaced rails fixed alternately to opposite faces of the posts. It looks the same from both sides. It is ideal for windy sites, since the gaps allow the wind to pass through the fence instead of blowing it down.*

**1** Build an interference fence from the bottom up. Attach the lowest rails, then pin a rail offcut to the side of the fence to act as a positional guide for the first rail on the other face of the post.

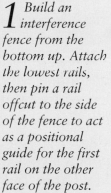

**2** Reposition the guide offcut and fix the next rail in place. Attach it with a single nail or screw and, using a spirit level, check that it is level and parallel with the first rail. Then complete the fixings.

**3** Once you have completed erecting the fence, give both the rails and posts a coat of preservative stain to protect them from rot and insect attack.

# Building a picket fence

Picket, or paling, fences are descended from medieval palisades, which were formed by driving pointed stakes into the ground to create a simple defensive barrier in battle or to pen in livestock. Their modern equivalents are made up as separate panels by nailing the pickets to two or three horizontal rails, which are then fixed to their supporting posts so that the lower ends of the pickets are held clear of the ground. The resulting fence is good-looking, especially if painted white and set against a backdrop of greenery such as a hedge, but it is not particularly secure and offers little privacy or protection against prevailing winds. You can obviously make the panels as high as you want, but picket fences are usually restricted to about 3ft(915mm) in height and are commonly used to fence front gardens, where appearance is more important than high security. The quickest way of making up the panels is to nail the rails to the pickets, but you can make the panels stronger if you use screws instead. Similarly, nailing the rails to the posts makes for fast fixing, but screws or simple wooden cleats around the ends of the rails will make the whole fence much sturdier. Whatever decorative finish you intend to use, it is vital to use wood that has been pretreated with preservative, since the exposed endgrain is vulnerable to water penetration and rot or insect attack. If you want a colored finish, use a microporous paint or stain that allows the wood to breathe.

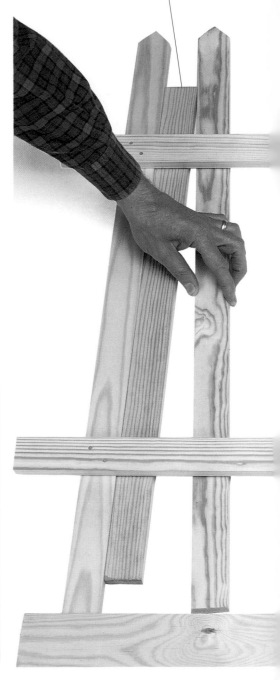

*You can use a narrower or wider spacer if you prefer.*

*A miter block or box will help you to cut accurate angles.*

*1 Start by cutting the pickets to shape. It is a good idea to prepare one 'master' picket and use it as a template for all the others to ensure that they are all the same shape.*

*2 Use a spacer to set the distance between the pickets as you fix them. Leave a gap between the first picket and the fence post and check that the picket is square to the rails.*

*3 Fix each rail to the picket with two galvanized nails, driven in on the diagonal to help resist twisting as you assemble the panel. You can use screws instead of nails if you prefer.*

*4 With the first picket attached to the rails, use the spacer again to set the position of the second picket. A baseboard acts as a handy guide to setting the pickets level.*

**5** *Leave the spacer in place as you drive in the nails for the next picket to ensure that each picket is parallel with the previous one.*

**6** *Fix the last picket in place. The rail should be long enough to fix to the post, leaving a picket's width gap between the last picket and the post.*

**7** *Support the completed panel on blocks between the posts. Nail the rails to the posts. Their ends should align with the center of the post.*

## Picket profiles

*The ends of the pickets can have any profile you wish. Here, simple semicircles have been cut with a jigsaw, which can easily cut more elaborate shapes, too. Always cut a master picket first, as a template for the rest.*

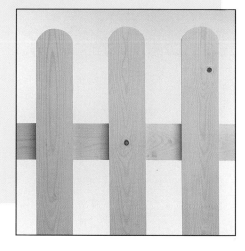

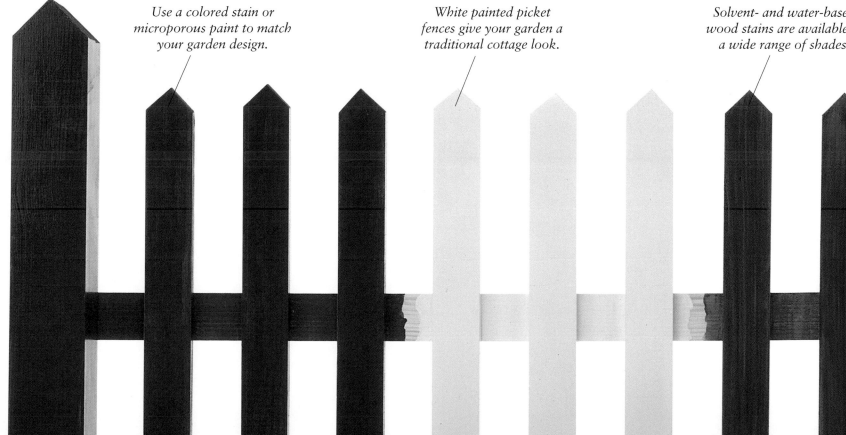

*Use a colored stain or microporous paint to match your garden design.*

*White painted picket fences give your garden a traditional cottage look.*

*Solvent- and water-based wood stains are available in a wide range of shades.*

# Garden fence options

The reason that wood is so widely used for all types of garden fencing is its sheer versatility. You can design and build a unique fence from scratch or adapt prefabricated fencing components to suit your requirements. Picket fencing and trelliswork in particular lend themselves to all sorts of creative, original designs. With picket fencing, for example, you can shape the ends of the pickets and assemble them into panels with shaped or undulating profiles as a change from endless straight lines. Nor does garden trelliswork have to feature the traditional square or diamond designs; with a little ingenuity you can create a range of unusual fan shapes and trompe l'oeil effects that will show off your plants to perfection. Remember, too, that other natural materials, such as bamboo canes and reeds, can be used to make up fence and screen panels if they are fixed within a sturdy wooden framework. Lastly, do not be put off using prefabricated fencing components by their limited range of standard sizes. A little simple carpentry is all it takes to cut them down to the precise size and shape you want for a particular application.

*Above:* To reduce the work involved in creating these delicately shaped pickets, make a master template first and then cut the marked-out copies with a power saw or router.

*Below:* There is virtually no limit to the shapes you can create with picket fencing, other than your own ingenuity. A preservative stain is the ideal finish for the precut pickets.

*Right:* This simple post-and-rail fence makes an economical and attractive boundary marker, but offers little in the way of security and privacy unless it is backed by dense planting.

## Shortening a fence panel

**1** You can seldom complete a run of prefabricated panel fencing with just whole panels. To cut one to size, start by levering off the two vertical edge battens from one side.

**2** Measure the width of panel you need to complete the run, pull out the old fixing nails and reposition the battens at the required distance from the opposite edge of the fence panel.

66

**Above:** Hurdles - sturdy frames inter-woven with slim branches of willow or other wood - were once used as temporary fencing for livestock. They make a perfect informal garden fence.

**Right:** If security is not of paramount importance, tall trellis panels securely mounted between fence posts and clothed with climbing plants make a green and pleasant screen.

**Left:** Unusual fencing materials, such as this panel of reeds, can make a striking backdrop for a collection of ornamental shrubs. The panels are simply stapled to the fence posts and arris rails behind.

**3** Drive new galvanized nails through the nail holes in the first batten, just penetrating the panel. Locate the second batten on the rear face of the panel and drive the nails fully home.

**4** Cut the panel to the required width by sawing off the waste wood next to the repositioned battens. Treat the bare wood with preservative stain before fixing the panel in place.

1 Having laid a suitable foundation, bed the first course of bricks in place. This two-step flight will use the face of the terrace wall as the final riser.

2 Start the second course by placing a half-brick at the rear of each side wall to maintain the stretcher bond. Tooth in a whole brick here if you are making a tall flight of steps.

3 Complete the second course with whole bricks. Use your spirit level to check that the bricks are truly horizontal and that their faces are vertical.

# Building brick steps

If your garden slopes steeply and is terraced, you will need to construct steps for access from one level to the next. These are more than simply functional; a well-designed flight of steps can be an important visual element in the overall landscaping plan. Construct them from materials that complement those used elsewhere in the garden for walls and paved surfaces. Bricks have a neat, formal look, while decorative stone walling blocks give a softer appearance. Paving slabs are ideal for forming the treads. Where you are linking two terraced areas, you can design the steps in a number of different ways. The flight can descend at right angles to the wall or be built parallel with it - often a better solution where one level is considerably higher than the other or where space is restricted on the lower level. A rectangular flight is the simplest to build, but you could create a series of semicircular steps instead. Bear in mind the dimensions of the materials you will be using when designing your steps. Treads and risers should be a standard size throughout the flight. Ideally, risers should be no more than about 180mm(7in) high - two bricks plus a paving slab is ideal - while treads should measure at least 305mm (12in) from front to back so that you do not catch your foot on the riser when climbing or descending the flight. Allowing the front of each tread to project slightly beyond the face of the riser beneath helps to make the edge of the tread clearly visible by casting a shadow on the riser.

Give the treads a very slight slope down towards the front edge to help drainage and to prevent puddles that could freeze in winter. Build the flight on proper foundations, just like any garden masonry structure; a continuous concrete slab slightly larger than the plan of the flight is the best solution. If it is more than two or three steps high, tie the structure to the wall against which it is being built to prevent the two from parting company if there is any movement of the subsoil. Use a process called toothing in, which involves removing a brick from alternate courses of the terrace wall so that one end of the corresponding whole brick in the side walls of the steps can be mortared into the structure.

**4** With the first course completed, build up internal supporting walls to carry the rest of the structure. You can use old bricks for this, and leave the vertical joints unpointed.

**5** Build up the brickwork for the second tread on top of the side and supporting walls. Add two more courses of internal brickwork to support the edges of the treads on the second step.

**6** Place the treads on the first step. Trowel on a generous mortar bed, lower the slabs into place and tamp them down so that they have a slight fall towards the front edge.

*To help provide a good grip in wet or wintry weather, choose slabs with a textured surface for steps.*

**7** Repeat the process for the second step. Then fill and point the joints between the pairs of slabs, and also the gaps at the rear of each tread.

**8** Complete the flight by bedding two slabs in place at the top of the flight, with their edges just projecting beyond the face of the terrace wall.

# Making rustic steps

Not all gardens are flat. Many contain gentle natural slopes, and some have banks between upper and lower levels that are too steep to walk up, either in comfort or safety, especially when the grass is wet. The solution is to construct steps in the bank, using the natural slope of the ground to support the flight. One way of doing this is to build risers of bricks or garden walling blocks, and to place paving slabs on top of the risers to create the individual treads as shown on pages 68-69. An alternative, particularly suited to the less formal garden, is to build wooden steps using round logs, sawn planks or even old railway ties (sleepers) if you can find a local source of supply. Whatever you use, the method is the same. The log, plank or tie forms the riser part of each step and is held in place with stout wooden pegs driven deep into the slope. You can then place further logs or ties behind each riser to form the individual treads, or fill the treads with a contrasting material, such as gravel or chipped bark. If you use a loose infill, edge the sides of each tread with nailed-on planks to create a box and prevent the infill from creeping out sideways. Since all the wood forming the steps is in permanent contact with the ground, it must be thoroughly protected against attack by rot or wood-boring insects. If possible, buy pretreated wood and brush more preservative onto all cut ends for extra protection.

## Treating wood

*You can buy stripped rustic logs from garden suppliers and cut them to the lengths you need. They will usually have been impregnated with preservative, but it is worth treating the cut ends with more preservative.*

*Treat the cut ends and apply the same preservative product to the rest of the log to give it a uniform color.*

*1 After deciding where you want to build the steps, carefully mark out the site using pegs, string lines and one of the riser logs as a width guide.*

*2 Use a garden spade to cut away the turf or other surface vegetation from the bank between the two string lines. Reuse or compost the turf.*

*3 Cut out the top of the bank so that the top riser will sit level with the grass. Create a smooth slope below this excavation.*

*4 Lay the bottom riser across the slope and secure it in place with two stout pegs driven vertically into the ground at each side.*

**7** Nail edging planks of sawn softwood to the sides of each tread to contain the gravel or bark infill. Make sure these are also treated with preservative.

**5** Place the next log riser on the slope and part-drive one fixing peg. Then use a batten and spirit level to position the riser accurately.

**6** When the underside of the second riser is level with the top of the first riser, drive a nail through each of the pegs into the logs.

*Each log in the flight is positioned so that its underside is level with the top edge of the log below it.*

**8** Peg and nail the other risers in position. With the edging planks nailed to the sides of the first tread, fill the space with gravel or bark chips.

*Preservative-treated stakes driven vertically into the ground support the ends of each log.*

**9** Complete the flight by adding edging planks to the sides of the other treads. Then fill and compact them with gravel or bark as before.

1 Erect two of the uprights at the recommended spacing. Check that they are truly vertical and that their notches are aligned. Lower one of the unnotched main side beams into the notches.

2 Adjust the position of the side beam so that it overhangs the uprights by an equal amount at each end. Drive a galvanized nail through the side of each post into the beam to lock it in place.

# Building a pergola

You can buy self-assembly pergolas in a range of sizes and styles from most garden centers and from mail-order fencing and outbuilding suppliers. All the parts are precut for simple and speedy assembly and the wood is pretreated to protect it from rot and insect attack. If you prefer to build a pergola to your own design, you can buy the wood - ideally pretreated with wood preservative - and cut it to size. Naturally, this is a cheaper option than buying a ready-to-assemble kit and gives you greater flexibility in matching the pergola's design and layout to your garden. Whichever method you choose, the most important part of the construction involves setting the uprights securely in the ground. You can use the techniques described on pages 54-55 for erecting fence posts, either using metal fence spikes driven into the ground or else setting roughly one quarter of the posts' length in concrete. The former method requires shorter (and hence cheaper) uprights, and also avoids the risk of rot since the post is held clear of the ground, but the latter provides a more permanent fixing.

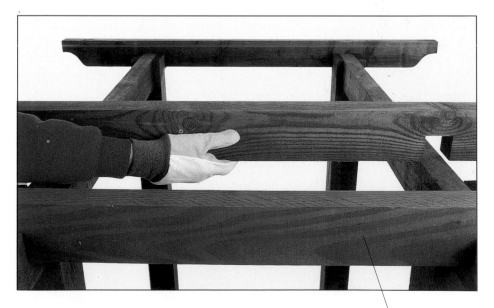

3 Build the opposite side of the pergola in the same way, taking care to position it so that the notched cross beams will fit precisely. Offer up the first cross beam near one end of the pergola.

4 Fit the second cross beam at the other end of the pergola, inset by the same distance as the first one. Fit the other two beams in the same way.

The spacing between the four cross beams should be the same.

Treat the trellis panels with a darker preservative stain if you want them to match the pergola.

**Left:** *A pergola really comes into its own when it is completely clothed in vegetation and can offer that uniquely dappled shade no manmade canopy can provide. Here a vine grows freely over the structure, which is flanked by conifers,* Berberis *and* Phormium *in a pot.*

Raise the trellis panels so that they are clear of rain splash and soil moisture.

5 *After checking that everything is correctly aligned, drive a nail down through each cross beam into the side beam to lock the structure securely.*

6 *Position the first trellis panel in between the two uprights, resting it on bricks to hold its bottom edge clear of the ground. Nail it to the uprights.*

7 *With the second trellis panel fixed in place on the opposite side of the structure, the pergola is complete and ready to support climbing plants.*

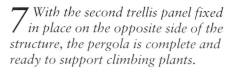

# Constructing a garden seat

Mention garden seats and many people think either of traditional wooden chairs and benches or of modern lightweight portable garden furniture. Both can be surprisingly expensive to buy. Portable items have to be set up before use and then stored away under cover when they are no longer required, while traditional pieces (usually left outdoors in all weathers) are becoming an increasingly popular target for thieves. One inexpensive, permanent and thief-proof solution is to build your own garden seating using bricks, mortar and preservative-treated wood. You can site a seat like this anywhere in your garden, but the best positions will allow you to catch the sun while you rest from your labors and admire the view - or the results of your hard work. This simple bench consists of two piers of brickwork, built without the need for any cut bricks, and a slatted seat that is screwed unobtrusively to the masonry to create a sturdy and good-looking garden structure that is surprisingly comfortable to use. You can build it directly on any existing paved or concrete surface; if you want to site it down the garden, set two paving slabs on some well-rammed subsoil to provide a stable base for the masonry. Choose bricks that match those used to build your house if you plan to site the seat close by - on the patio, for example. If you prefer to build it further down the garden, you could use garden walling blocks instead to create a seat with a more rustic appearance. The seat can be left with a natural finish (protected by clear preservative to protect it from rot and insect attack), or can be stained or painted if you prefer a colored finish.

*1 Build up the piers, positioning two bricks side by side and a third at right angles to them in each course. Check that each face is truly vertical.*

*2 Decide on the width of the bench and build up the second pier in the same way. Use a spirit level on a timber straightedge to check that the two piers are precisely level with each other.*

*3 Cut two seat support blocks from 2in(50mm) square softwood, slightly longer than the depth of the piers. Fix one to the outside face of each pier with screws and wallplugs.*

*4 Cut two seat edge slats to length and attach them to the ends of the seat support blocks. The overlap at each end helps to conceal the support blocks when the bench is completed.*

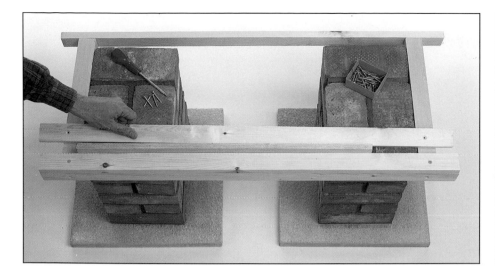

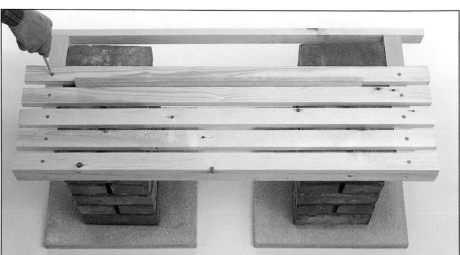

**5** *Screw on the first seat slat so that it rests on top of the front edge slat and forms a neat angle. Use a spacer slat on edge to position the next slat. Countersink all the screw heads.*

*Round off the edges of the slats with sandpaper to prevent splinters.*

**6** *Continue fixing the slats to the seat support blocks, using your spacer slat to ensure even gaps. Use one predrilled slat as a pattern for drilling the screw holes in the others.*

## Other styles

*The design shown here is ideal for a garden seat because rainwater can drain away freely between the slats. However, if you prefer a solid seat, simply close up the gaps between the slats, and glue each one to its neighbor with waterproof woodworking adhesive before you screw it to the supporting framework. If you want to make a longer seat, space the piers accordingly, increase the depth of the two seat edge slats to 3in (75mm) and use thicker wooden slats for the rest of the seat to prevent it from sagging.*

**7** *With the final slats screwed in place, the seat is ready for use. Apply two coats of clear preservative to keep rot and insect attack at bay or use paint or stain if you prefer a colored finish to the natural look.*

*If you are using slabs as supports, compact the subsoil well and bed them onto some sand so that you can level them easily.*

# Seating in the garden

No garden should be without some sort of seating, whether it is formal or informal. Gardeners deserve a rest from their labors from time to time, and visitors will appreciate the opportunity to sit and admire your handiwork. The type of seating you choose will depend on your taste and on the style of the garden. You may want to create simple bench seats in out-of-the-way corners, or to make the seating a major feature of your garden design. Whichever option you select, wood is the ideal material because it is easy to work, warm and comfortable to sit on and dries off quickly after rain. However, durable hardwoods are expensive and cheaper softwood is prone to rot unless it has been treated with preservative and is well maintained. If you choose wood, you can build seating to your own plans or buy prefabricated benches and seats and design the garden layout round them. The simpler styles - a plank on two posts, for example - are ideal for taking a short breather while you work. More ornate types, with backs and arm rests, are for the serious lounger.

Masonry seats are formed from paving slabs incorporated into raised planters and retaining walls, but stone is cold and retains moisture, so is best regarded as a summer seat surface. Whatever type of seat you choose, position it carefully so that it forms an integral part of the garden design as well as providing a pleasant viewpoint.

## A seat around a tree

**1** Buying a prefabricated tree seat avoids the need for fairly complex carpentry. Treat the seat with a preservative stain before assembling it.

**2** Use curved moulded edging stones as a sturdy base for the legs. Lay them on the ground next to the tree and cut round them with a trowel.

**3** Cut away the turf, compact the subsoil and lay a bed of sand in the excavation. Put each stone in position and tamp it down to get it level.

**Above:** There is room for a simple plank seat in even the smallest garden. The uprights can simply be hammered into the ground; the seat is nailed on.

**Left:** A small gap left in this earth-retaining stockade allows the inclusion of a simple paving slab seat. It rests on shorter posts at the front and back.

**Right:** At the opposite extreme is this stunning swing seat, supported by an unusual triangular-shaped pergola and surrounded by easy-care gravel.

6 The assembled seat turns a bare tree trunk into an attractive garden feature. Seats are available in various sizes to enable you to match a range of different tree diameters.

4 Stand the first prefabricated seat section in place on its stones, then offer up the second section. Raise or lower the stones slightly as necessary.

5 Thread the bolts through the predrilled holes. Add another washer before fitting the nut so that it does not bite into the wood.

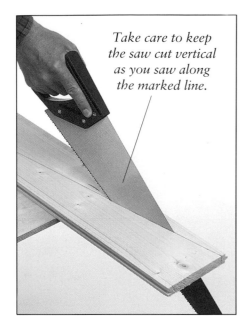

*Take care to keep the saw cut vertical as you saw along the marked line.*

# Building a cold frame

A cold frame is a useful addition to any garden. It is basically a bottomless box with a glazed lid and is used like a miniature greenhouse to grow seeds and cuttings and to acclimatize tender plants that have been raised under cover before they are finally planted out in the garden. It can stand on a hard surface, such as a patio or path - the best idea if you intend to fill it with seed trays and plant pots - or can be placed directly on the soil so that you can plant things in it. You can buy ready-made cold frames, but making your own is a simple and satisfying project that allows you to tailor-make the frame to just the size you want. You can make the cold frame entirely from softwood, or build up the base in brickwork and add a wooden-framed lid. The lid can be glazed with glass, but plastic glazing materials are safer and easier to work with. Hinge it to the base so that you can open it during the day for ventilation and fit a simple catch to the front edge to keep it closed at night; strong winds could lift and damage it otherwise. If you want a larger planting and growing area than a single frame provides, simply add further bays to the basic structure as the need arises. Site the completed frame in a sunny position, ideally sheltered from the prevailing winds, and keep the lid clean to allow the maximum amount of sunlight to reach the plants inside. Cover it on cold nights with sacking or some old carpet to cut down on heat loss.

*1 Cut the planks that will form the front, back and sides of the frame to the desired length. Mark angled cutting lines on the two top side boards and cut carefully along them.*

*4 Cut the back legs to match the height of two full boards plus the thicker end of the top side board. Continue to build up the box; attach the second set of boards all round.*

*2 Cut front legs to match the height of two full boards, plus the thinner end of the top side board. Drill clearance holes in the boards. Screw the bottom two boards to one leg.*

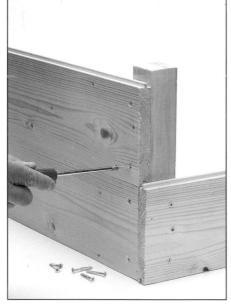

*3 Interlock the grooved edge of the second full board over the tongue on the first board. Tap it down along its length to close up the joint fully. Screw the board to the leg as before.*

**5** *Offer up the two tapered top side boards, interlocking the tongued and grooved edges as before. Attach them to the legs with two screws at the back and one screw at the front.*

**6** *Cut down the top back board to match the height of the thicker end of the tapered top side boards. Make sure that the waste wood you remove includes the tongued edge of the board. Plane or sand the cut edge.*

*The four legs of the frame are cut to length from 2in (50mm) square softwood.*

*Secure the boards to the legs with 1½in(38mm) countersunk screws.*

*The sloping side section is cut so its grooved edge fits over the tongue of the plank below.*

*Use plated or galvanized screws to avoid rust marks.*

*The frame sides are made up from interlocking lengths of 6 x ¾in(150x19mm) tongued and grooved cladding.*

**7** *Cut down another board in the same way to create a narrow strip the same height as the thinner end of the top side boards. Screw it to the front legs to complete the base of the cold frame.*

# The cold frame lid

**3** Lay the assembled frame over the glazing material - this is twin-wall polycarbonate, a tough and rigid translucent plastic sheet. Use a felt-tipped pen to mark the cutting lines clearly.

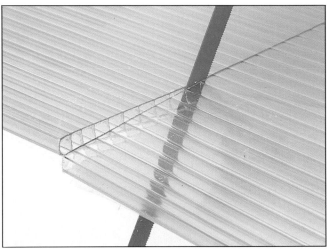

**4** Cut the sheet to size. To cut across it, use a fine-toothed saw, such as a hacksaw blade fitted in a padsaw handle. Make cuts that run parallel to the internal ribs with a sharp knife.

**1** Measure the width and depth of the cold frame base as your first step towards constructing the glazed lid for the frame. Make it from 1x2in (25x50mm) planed softwood.

**2** Cut the components to size. The two side pieces overlap the cut ends of the front and back pieces. Drill and counterbore holes for fixing screws; glue and screw the frame together.

*5* Glue and screw strips of 1x2in (25x50mm) softwood to the side edges of the lid to protect the edges of the polycarbonate sheet and cover the corner fixing screws.

*6* Lay the lid in place on top of the base to fit the hinges. Position them about 9in(230mm) in from the corners, and attach them with ¾in (19mm)-long countersunk screws.

*7* Treat the frame and lid with two coats of preservative stain and leave it to dry with the lid propped open. Check that the brand of stain you buy is not harmful to plants.

You can buy special tape for sealing the cut edges of polycarbonate sheet.

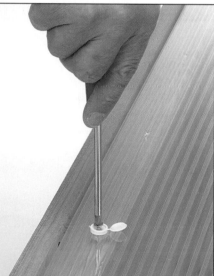

*8* When the stain is dry, place the polycarbonate sheet on the lid and drill clearance holes through it at intervals. Screw it down, using plastic screw cups with snap-on covers.

*9* Complete the screw fixings all round and check that all the screw caps are snapped firmly in place. Use two small softwood offcuts to prop the lid open for ventilation.

This green preservative is safe for use with plants.

# Making a wooden planter

Planting in above-ground containers has many advantages over in-ground gardening. For a start, you can work from a standing rather than a kneeling position, which is a boon for the elderly or partly disabled. Whatever you decide to plant is self-contained, allowing you to keep over-vigorous growth from spreading too far. Weeds are easy to keep under control, if they ever get a chance to thrive at all in a well-stocked container. You can move the container around if you wish, placing it in sunshine or shelter as necessary. Groups of containers can also be an ideal way of breaking up the featureless expanse of a large patio. You can use all kinds of containers, but wooden planters are some of the most versatile. You can make them in virtually any shape and size, from a slimline windowbox to a large ornamental square or rectangular display centerpiece, using the technique shown here. Tongued-and-grooved cladding is an ideal material for the planter's sides; you simply use as many planks as are necessary to give the height of container you want, and you can easily remove the tongue from the topmost planks to leave a neat square edge. Internal posts form the corners of the container, and the removable base panel sits on battens fixed to the inner face of the side walls. A series of drainage holes bored in the base panel allows the planter to drain freely in wet weather or after watering.

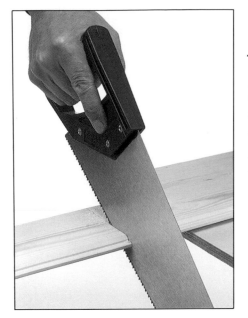

*1 Decide on the overall dimensions of the planter you want to make and cut enough lengths of cladding to form the four sides. Sand the cut ends smooth to remove any splinters.*

*2 Assemble the sides by interlocking the edges of the planks. It is best to glue them together as well, using waterproof woodworking adhesive. Squeeze some into the grooves.*

*3 Assemble the planks to form each side, using a hammer and a cladding offcut to knock them tightly together. If any excess adhesive oozes out, wipe it off with a damp cloth.*

*4 Make up the short ends of the planter first. Cut two corner posts for each end, then glue and nail the assembled side panels to the posts with the tongued edge uppermost.*

*5 Use two nails per plank, punching the nail heads just below the surface of the wood. You can disguise the holes with exterior-grade wood filler when assembly is complete.*

6 Rest the base of the planter on slim battens glued and pinned to the inner faces of the side walls, flush with their bottom edges. Cut and fix the two battens to the assembled end walls of the planter first.

7 Place one of the assembled long side walls of the planter on a flat surface and stand the two completed ends next to it so that their faces are aligned with the ends of the side wall. Measure the distance between the corner posts.

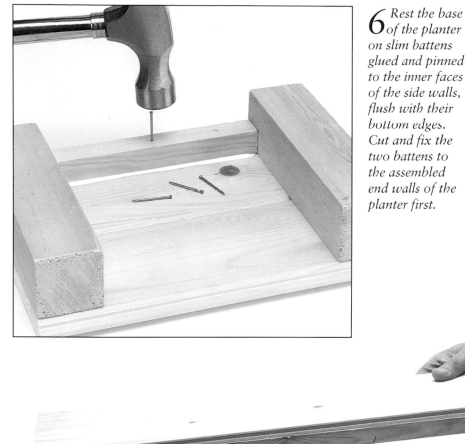

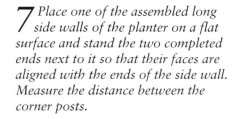

Cut and fix the support battens to the inner faces of the two long side panels, in the same way as described in step 6.

8 Assemble the planter by gluing the side walls to the two end sections. Using just adhesive at this stage allows you to align the corner joints and check that the whole assembly is square.

9 Once you have made any adjustments, leave the adhesive to set for a while. Nail the side walls to the corner posts and punch in the nail heads as described in steps 4 and 5.

**1** *To mark the outline of the planter base, stand the planter upside down on the plywood sheet and draw carefully round the internal profile of the planter walls with a pencil.*

*Always use exterior-grade plywood for the planter base; anything else will rot.*

# Adding the finishing touches

Once you have assembled the planter walls, it is time to fit the base - a piece of exterior-grade plywood. Although this fits fairly loosely within the planter, drill some extra drainage holes through it to prevent the contents from becoming waterlogged. You can leave the upper tongued edges of the cladding exposed if you wish; to conceal them, plane them off or add cut-down strips of cladding as shown here. With the planter complete, apply two coats of a microporous paint or woodstain, which will not flake and peel as time goes by. Place a pebble over each drainage hole to prevent them from becoming blocked and fill the planter with a suitable planting mixture. If you intend to use your planter as a windowbox, either stand it on the sill if this is wide enough, using wedges to get it level, or make up some simple triangular brackets from spare wood and screw these to the wall to support the box.

**2** *Extend the pencil lines so that they meet at each corner and cut out the resulting rectangle. Then use a tenon saw to remove the small square of waste wood at each corner to allow the base to fit round the posts.*

**3** *Make a series of equally-spaced holes in the base using a flat wood bit in your power drill. Drill through into some scrap wood to ensure that the edges of the holes do not splinter as the bit bursts through.*

**4** *Simply drop the plywood base into the planter so that it rests on the support battens on the inner faces of the planter walls. You can pin and glue it in place if you prefer, although this is not essential.*

**5** One way of finishing off the top edges of the planter's sides neatly is to cut down some narrow strips of the cladding and glue their grooved edges to the exposed tongues, as shown here.

**Right:** You can set a small planter on wall brackets beneath a window if you wish. Space the brackets so that they support the corner posts of the planter and screw them to the planter for safety's sake, especially if it is fixed at a high level.

**6** You can leave the planter undecorated so long as you have made it from preservative-treated wood. Otherwise, finish it with two coats of microporous paint or wood stain in the colour of your choice.

# Making a bird table

For much of the year, the birds that visit your garden will find their own food - either on the ground or on the plants you grow. Watching them can add an extra dimension to the pleasure your garden gives you, and you will be surprised at the number of different species it will attract. However, putting up a bird table will make it much easier for you to observe their feeding habits, and in winter it will provide a welcome boost to their scarce food supply. It does not need to be an elaborate structure, just a simple platform with a raised lipping all round to stop food blowing off the surface, and you can probably make one up from scrap wood lying around your workshop. This table is made from a square of exterior-grade plywood with some 1in(25mm) square planed softwood pinned on round its perimeter. It is a good idea to leave a small gap at one corner so you can brush away uneaten food easily from time to time. It is secured to its post by screws driven through two supporting blocks of scrap wood on its underside, and is finished with water-based preservative wood stain. You can add hooks round the edges for suspended feeders to increase its versatility. You can also make the bird table free-standing if you wish by adding some simple feet to the post, but such a structure will be easily toppled on windy days. It will be more stable if you let it into a socket set in the ground (see panel).

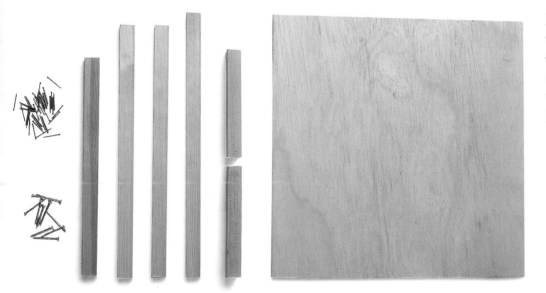

*1 To make a bird table like this, you will need a square of exterior-grade plywood, four lengths of 1in(25mm) square softwood for the lipping, two 1x2in(25x50mm) offcuts for the supporting blocks and a post, plus some panel pins and countersunk screws.*

*The post can be planed or sawn wood. If you intend to set it in a hole in the ground, soak its bottom end in wood preservative first.*

*2 Cut the lipping to length and fix it in place by pinning the plywood base to each length in turn. Leave the final length of lipping shorter than the other pieces.*

**3** Find the center of the base by drawing its diagonals. Then lay the post across the centre of the base and place the supporting blocks either side of it. Mark their positions, then drill clearance holes through the plywood.

**4** Fix the supporting blocks securely to the underside of the bird table. Apply some waterproof woodworking adhesive to one edge of each block and press it into place, aligning it carefully with the pencil lines.

**5** Turn the table base over and drive screws through each of the four clearance holes into the supporting blocks beneath. Countersink the screw heads slightly.

**6** Position the post between the two blocks and use a try square to check that the top and post are at right angles to each other. Drive two screws through each block into the post.

**7** Give the table two coats of water-based preservative wood stain to protect it and make it easier to clean. Allow this to dry thoroughly before setting the table up in your garden.

**8** Put out a variety of food to attract a range of different bird species. You can buy mixed nuts and seeds from pet shops and garden centers everywhere. Add hanging feeders, too, if you wish, suspended from hooks round the edge of the table.

# Making a nest box

However your garden is planted, it will always attract birds. In their quest for food they help to rid the garden of many insect pests, and their presence, however temporary, is always a visual pleasure. If you want to persuade them to stay a little longer, try offering them some secure accommodation. Do not worry about the quality of the architecture; birds nest in the most extraordinary places, so a nesting box that looks like the Taj Mahal will not impress them. All they require is a simple box that provides shelter from the elements and protection from predators. It needs a simple sloping roof to help shed rainwater and a hole in the front to let the parents in and the offspring out. The diameter of the hole will help to determine which species use the box, so select it to favor those that visit your garden most regularly. Where you site it matters little, so long as it is securely fixed and gives the birds a degree of privacy. It is best not to put it too near the house or close to where you feed birds in the garden. Once it is occupied, do not disturb it until the fledglings have flown. Then remove the lid and take out the old nest, which can harbor pests and will discourage future occupants.

Use a strip of softwood or plywood about 6in(150mm) wide.

**1** Mark out the components of the box on a strip of softwood or plywood. This box will measure about 8in(200mm) high at the front and 10in(250mm) at the back.

**2** Cut the four sides and the base of the box to length with a panel or tenon saw. Support the offcut as you complete each cut to prevent the wood from splintering.

**3** Mark the position for the entrance hole on the front panel, about 2in (50mm) below the top edge, and drill it out with a flat wood bit to the size you have chosen.

The roof is a piece of exterior-grade plywood that overlaps all round.

Side panel

Side panel

Back panel

Entrance hole

Front panel

Drill a small hole in the center of the base for drainage.

Use galvanized nails to assemble the nest box

**5** Start by nailing the back wall to the edge of the base. Raise the underside of the base just above the bottom edge of the wall to protect its endgrain.

**6** Chamfer off the top edge of the back wall to match the slope of the side walls. Use one of these to mark the angle, then remove the waste wood with a plane or planer file.

**7** Check the alignment of the tops of the side walls with the chamfered edge of the back wall. Nail on the sides; punch the nail heads in slightly.

**9** Screw an offcut to the rear wall of the box. You can then drive nails or screws through this support to fix the box in position - easier than making fixings through the back wall of the box itself.

**8** Slide the front wall into place with its top edge level with the tops of the side walls. Drive nails through the side walls into the front wall. Then nail it to the front edge of the base.

**10** Attach the plywood roof panel to the support fitted in step 9, using a small rustproof hinge and matching screws. Check that these do not pierce the plywood on the inside.

**11** Use a small hook-and-eye catch to keep the roof securely closed in windy weather. Fit the eye to the underside of one edge of the roof, and the hook to the side of the box.

**12** Treat the outside of the completed box with a coat of water-based wood stain if you wish. Allow it to dry thoroughly before securing it in its chosen location.

# Index

# Credits

The majority of the photographs featured in this book have been taken by Neil Sutherland and are ©
Colour Library Books. The publishers wish to thank the following photographers for providing
additional photographs, credited here by page number and position on the page, i.e. (B)Bottom, (T)Top,
(C)Center, (BL)Bottom left, etc.

Eric Crichton: Half-title, contents page, 16(T), 22-23(B), 25(BR), 28(BL), 29(TR), 31(BR),
33(L,TR,BR), 38(BL), 39(TR), 61(BR) 66(T), 67(TL), 76(T)
John Glover: 19(BL,BR), 28(BR), 35(TR), 47(TR), 85(TR)
S & O Mathews: 67(TC)
Natural Image: 38(R), 45(TR)
Clive Nichols: 10 (Richard Coward, designer), 17(BL, Old Rectory, Northants.), 27(T, Jean Bishop,
designer), 27(BR, Keeyla Meadows, San Francisco), 32(T, Woking Borough Council),
32(B, The Anchorage, Kent), 39(TL, Richard Coward, designer), 67(TR, Bourton House, Glos.),
67(BR, Graham Strong, designer), 73(TL, Jill Billington, designer) 77(TL, Richard Coward, designer),
77(TR, Paula Rainey-Crofts, designer)

## Acknowledgments

The publishers would like to thank the following people and organizations for their help during the
preparation of this book: Forest Fencing Ltd.; Garboldisham Garden Center; Hillhout; Millbrook
Garden Center, Gravesend; Murrells Nurseries, Pulborough; Sharpe and Fisher Building Supplies,
Pulborough; Thakeham Tiles Ltd., Timber World, Horsham; Travis Perkins Trading
Company Ltd., Crawley.